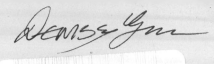

Subcultural Sounds

MUSIC / CULTURE

A series from Wesleyan University Press

Edited by George Lipsitz, Susan McClary, and Robert Walser

Published titles

My Music by Susan D. Crafts, Daniel Cavicchi, Charles Keil,
and the Music in Daily Life Project

*Running with the Devil: Power, Gender, and Madness in
Heavy Metal Music* by Robert Walser

Subcultural Sounds: Micromusics of the West by Mark Slobin

MARK SLOBIN

❖

Subcultural Sounds

MICROMUSICS

OF THE WEST

❖

WESLEYAN UNIVERSITY PRESS

Published by University Press of New England

Hanover & London

WESLEYAN UNIVERSITY PRESS
Published by University Press of New England, Hanover, NH 03755
© 1993 by Mark Slobin
All rights reserved
Printed in the United States of America 5 4 3 2 1
CIP data appear at the end of the book

An earlier version of much of the material included in this book
was published as "Micromusics of the West: A Comparative
Approach" in *Ethnomusicology* 36:1 (Winter 1992), and is hereby
reprinted with the permission of the University of Illinois Press.
Lyrics to "Bicentennial Polka" used by permission from Ray Henry.

To all the good friends,
from Kabul to California, 1967–92

Contents

❖

Preface

❖

I began my work as an ethnomusicologist in Afghanistan in 1967, and moved slowly eastward through Europe to the United States. Everywhere I went I noticed small musics living in big systems. Groups of people in neighborhoods, in clusters across entire countries, or even in diaspora seem to think that certain musical styles, instruments, songs, ways of singing or playing, ideas about what music is or might be, were somehow "ours." And what's "ours" was always set apart from what's not: "mine," "theirs," or "everybody's."

This fascinating counterpoint of near and far, large and small, neighborhood and national, home and away, has haunted me as I work on specialized situations in particular places. Nowhere is it safe to draw conclusions about what belongs to whom, because it isn't how the music *sounds*, but how it can be *thought* that counts: outsiders—even if certified by doctorates in music—all have tin ears. Below, I intend to tell you how studying small musics fits into current debates and disciplines, including those of my own field, ethnomusicology, but here I just want to talk about how tangled music really is. Let me offer three metaphors:

1. *Homespun*. We are all individual music cultures, using patchworks of compiled sounds stitched into a cultural quilt to help keep us warm. But we are restless sleepers; from time to time we throw off the covers, change the linen, look for sleeping pills, or even buy an electric blanket, which leads us to:

2. *Electronic*. Our musical antennae are always waving about in the atmosphere, ignoring some sounds and hauling in others for future reference, although we still don't have a clue as to how we do so or why. We have stored away countless live and recorded sounds, tied to kin, friends, moments, and often the music triggers the memories rather than the

other way round. Yet we are not freestanding, factory-fresh equipment; *contexts* matters to us as much as inputs, which takes us to:

3. *Environmental.*   Amid a set of personal landscapes we can identify formations, musical Stonehenges, that stand free and look communal. Like that ancient pile, such structures are cryptic, mutely posing puzzles of who shaped them and what they represent. Unlike those changeless megaliths, musical monuments are mobile, flexible, more like a mirage. The nearer you get, the more their rigid outlines shift in the shimmering air. Less poetically, what I mean is that we make temporary shelters of our musical materials, not only personally, but collectively. Up close, what's "Irish," "American," or "Irish-American" looks like the work of tent-dwellers, not stone-raisers after all.

I'm collecting metaphors here to make a point that I'll keep returning to below: we need to think of music as coming from many places and moving among many levels of today's societies, just as we have learned to think of groups and nations as volatile, mutable social substances rather than as fixed units for instant analysis. Yet at any moment, we can see music at work in rather specific ways, creating temporary forcefields of desire, belonging, and, at times, transcendence.

Let me get away from metaphors and down to cases, of which Andy Statman's might make the point. When I first met Andy in the late 1970s, he had just switched over from being a leading mandolinist in bluegrass/newgrass music to helping found the fledgling *klezmer* movement. This movement was a drive by younger Jewish-American musicians of differing pasts and persuasions to forge a new "ethnic" style based on their neglected "Jewish" roots. Fifteen years later, the *New York Times* (April 12, 1992) finds Statman in "a home resonant with delightful sounds" as "a man of many talents and strong [Orthodox Jewish] faith." Meanwhile, his music has branched out past the older *klezmer* sound to include not only his old favorite, bluegrass, but beyond. As Statman says, "the orchestra plays traditional Jewish European music, but we also flow freely into bits and pieces of what we like. . . . It's our own form of improvisation, and folk music and the bluegrass influence is right there." "Indeed," says the reporter, "his music is so varied he jokingly calls it 'Moroccan African Mongolian klezmer music.'" In figuring out this stance, remember that the "traditional Jewish European music" itself was a blend of styles including Moldavian, Ukrainian, and shades of Balkan, all transformed in New York in the 1920s and 30s.

Even a brief attempt at understanding Andy Statman shows us: (1) any essentialist analysis of music will not hold; (2) interchange among small musics is rampant these days, and always was; (3) musicians, like the rest of us, negotiate individuality in very complex ways (here the process involves an unpredictable knotting of aesthetics, professionalism, and multiple allegiances); (4) units like Statman's orchestra are the fulcrum on which individual and group identities turn and balance precariously in the cultural and subcultural winds.

The point of the following essays is emphatically *not* to make sense of the iceberg of which Statman is the tip—I would rapidly run aground—but rather to try out ways of systematic viewing. Only by pretending that things are stable can we see how they change. Above all, I will be interested in *interaction*, within small groups, between social groupings, and with the powers that be (industry and ideology, bureaucrats and bankers) that set the tone, make the rules, and provide the resources. There are no "simple" societies any longer, yet "complex" is too flat a word to describe the nestings and foldings, the cracks and crannies of the lands of Euro-America. All I propose to do is sketch out a framework for further thought, which we will badly need in this time of radical reshaping, after the collapse of the East-West structure that defined the political, economic, and human landscape of the region for two generations. After all, if there is no Second World (never clearly defined or analyzed anyway), we need no longer speak of a "First" and "Third" World. The "advanced" North Atlantic area has turned out to be as confused as the "developing" or "backwards" zones it once defined by supposed superiority. Meanwhile, the fragmenting and regluing of the eastern zones proceeds fitfully and unpredictably. Overall, the music of Euro-America in the 1990s is at least as complicated as that of any-place on the planet, especially since Euro-America is the place to which much of the rest of the world has moved or longs to migrate. In transit, in process, and even in their dreams they all sing—or at least wear headphones to mask exterior noise with interior sounds.

This is a good place to thank a number of Central European colleagues for helpful discussions undertaken under an American Council of Learned Societies Grant-in-Aid trip in 1984; Soviet colleagues, particularly Eduard Alekseev, for creating conditions for fruitful interchanges at the three meetings of the IREX Commission on Musicology, Ethnomusicology, Music Composition and Jazz (1987, 1988, 1989); Owe Ronström, Anders Hammerlund, Krister Malm, and other Swedish colleagues for a fine reception and working sessions in Sweden in 1988 and 1990; Ankica Petrovic for hospitality in Yugoslavia in 1988; Wesleyan University for sabbatical time in 1990; the University of California at Santa Cruz through Frederic Lieberman for research associate status, and Jim Clifford, Center for Cultural Studies; Kay K. Shelemay for a helpful reading of a draft; Dick Ohmann for sessions at the Center for Humanities at Wesleyan; graduate students at Wesleyan over twenty-one years for pushing my thinking and keeping me going; Jeff Titon for accepting the original version in *Ethnomusicology*; Maya Slobin for copyediting and just for being her own sweet self; and Greta Slobin for not only (literally) surviving but also providing a place in the sun where my thoughts fell into place.

July 1992   M.S.

PART ONE

❖

FRAMING THE
PROJECT

❖

Opening Thoughts

❖

Of late, anthropology has been telling itself to look inward, in terms of both fieldwork at home and the ethnographer's self as the field. Meanwhile, cultural theorists have urged a broader view, pushing toward the study of "global cultural flow" and going beyond ethnography toward seeing local scenes as inseparable from a media-driven, internal fantasy life that takes people's minds far from native grounds (see Fox 1991, a helpful anthology covering both trends).

Those of us who study world music have long since bumped into the on-the-ground reality that drive such recommendations. Trying to study village and town musics in Afghanistan in the period 1967–72, I first had to elbow aside, then recognize the power of, radio music emanating from Kabul, the capital. My work in the Afghan north ended up centering on issues of intense localism versus general patterns, for both geography (town-to-town variation) and ethnicity (in-group versus shared patterns). And this was in a land where global cultural flow was a mere trickle at best. When I moved to then-Soviet Central Asia to place Afghan peoples in a broader social context, to Eastern European venues to understand Jewish traditions, and finally to the United States to study immigrant musical patterning, the sheer complexity of the shifting contexts for music-making forced me to look for frameworks of analysis that the literature did not seem to offer. Somehow, the same problems kept cropping up across a vast landscape of musics, peoples, and places, and eventually it seemed possible to halt my march and take a stand; this book is part of that decision.

The work process made me realize that one "is the field" in a way that's slightly different from the usual understanding of that phrase. Normally it means that one's perception of the Other, in a given ethnographic site, is inevitably locked into one's own perspective. More broadly, it is said that we of the West can only view the Rest in limited, biased ways. I have no quarrel with this general insight, but I think it offers a partial view. Whether studying current communities abroad, the Lower East Side of New York at the turn of the twentieth century, or local musical scenes in contemporary America, I have gravitated toward similar issues, to seek the same framework regardless of whether the group is Other or Self (Jewish-Americans from Eastern Europe). This type of personal perspective, translated into methodological suggestions below, represents a meeting ground between my own needs as researcher/writer and what I think the "field"—here understood in its other sense as the community of scholars—needs to think about, since I have both internalized and tried to decenter myself from my discipline. Both meanings of "field" shape the imaginary landscape onto which I project the following essays.

One is never totally reflexive—it would be too eccentric. We locate ourselves between the people we work on and the people we work with. The more the two converge, the more our position is revealed. Studying the American cantorate was particularly piquant—my "informants" looked like me, came from, lived in, and worked in similar neighborhoods, earned about the same salary, and wrote twelve-page reviews in their journals of the book I produced about them. Yet my interests and theirs diverged so substantially that I felt little strain.

I am playing out this line of thought simply to position what follows as a reflective, but not ostentatiously reflexive, extended essay. Let me turn from myself as field to why I think the larger field has left me the opening I'm stepping into here.

The study of world musics moved out of what would nowadays be called an Orientalist stance only in the 1960s. Till then, few people seriously questioned the notion that beyond the Western classical tradition there were three kinds of music to be studied: Oriental, folk, and primitive. This triad underlaid many works and was implicit in the training of my generation of researchers. "Oriental" of course referred to those Asian "high cultures" that had long-term, accessible internal histories and that could be "compared" with similar European systems. "Primitive" encompassed all the "preliterate" peoples of the world, who had to rely on oral tradition for transmission and who had no highly professionalized "art musicians" in their midst. The "folk" were the internal primitives of Euro-America.

The 1970s saw a dramatic breakdown of this model because of a few key developments. The rapid spread of sound-producing technologies led to the formation of global media networks that accelerated the normal intercultural spread of musics. Somewhat before anthropology was willing to concede the lessening importance of purely local scenes (Appadurai and Abu-Lughod in Fox 1991), ethnomusicologists conceded that acknowledging interactive patterns of various sorts was crucial to their work: the musicians taught us what our advisors had overlooked. At the same time, scholars like myself started researching nearby communities for a variety of reasons, ranging from the post-imperialist booting out of scholars from foreign lands to the intellectual and personal drive for seeing what it would be like to study the Self—however defined—after regarding the Other. Meanwhile, our colleagues from abroad stopped being quite so Other as the frame of reference widened. Finally, we became aware of emerging metadisciplines that were abandoning such concepts as "innate structures of the mind" or inevitable stages of social evolution. Instead, we were told to look for fluid, ambiguous relationships of power within societies and for overarching linkages across borders. For me, it seemed that ethnomusicology had been set free, allowed finally to make its proper contribution to discourse about culture, now understood less as sets of rules than as relationships. In this new interpretation, expression, imagination, and fantasy move toward center stage in the now archaic-sounding "sciences of man."

But what our contribution as music observers might be to such a de-centered intellectual scene and within our own lineage of learning has remained indistinct. As usual, we can point to a number of influential first-start examples. Roger Wallis and Krister Malm's 1984 delineation of the international phonogram industry's relationship to "small countries" made the point that both Sweden and Jamaica could be handled under the same rubric in terms of the way commercial giants operate. For all its limitations, Peter Manuel's 1988 pioneering attempt to span global popular music was another step in the direction of broadened context. Both works exceed the general description of the discipline offered in the last general survey (Nettl 1983). For my own part, in the late seventies and early eighties I had a hard time situating the Jewish-American case in a hoped-for literature about immigration, ethnic identity, or the evolution of popular culture among what are usually called subcultures in Europe and North America. Even placing the group's internal sheet music industry within a nationwide context was a pipe dream—popular music *systems*, as opposed to stars, songs, or trends, were (and remain) largely unstudied. As articles on "ethnic" musics appeared through the 1980s, I took some comfort in their descriptions, but still saw no attempt at an overview; each author seemed to reinvent the basic music-cultural context. To suit the material at hand, every study offered an idiosyncratic set of analytical terms and tools. Hence the present effort to suggest frameworks, guidelines, categories that are general enough to imply the emergence of a future comparative method and open-ended enough to allow for substantial revision and extension.

A parallel and encouraging trend has emerged as colleagues in various fields of study have begun routinely to make reference to music—if only in terms of iconic figures like Madonna—naturally and frequently as part of their current discourse. But it might be worth a brief outlining of the place of music in the world covered by the following chapters.

We ethnomusicologists like to be sentimental about music, the subject of our labors and provider of our pleasures. We celebrate its ubiquity in all societies and times, its ability to create transcendent, euphoric states among music-makers from ritual groups through singing circles. We note with satisfaction everyone's need, regardless of background, to have *some* kind of music at weddings. We might fondly quote the old German saying *Wo Menschen singen lass dich ruhig nieder / Denn böse Menschen singen keine Lieder* ("Where people are singing rest easy/Since bad people sing no songs"). Yet we also pull back to a more neutral notion of the centrality of music when observing, say, the long-running Israeli debate over the performance of Wagner. Few of us are likely to agree with Leonard Bernstein's crack that without the words, the Nazi's *Horst Wessel* song is just another nice tune. Conceding the possibility of an alliance between evil and music—after all, it demonstrates the power of music—we are perhaps more unsettled by the sheer banality of music in contemporary life, from the dentist's office to the vapid video hit that privileges the visual over the aural. If music can be either intensively expressive or numbingly neutral, a rallying cry for both the good guys and the bad, we have to contextualize it differently than we would if it were always positive—the latter model being a leftover from our early days as crusaders for cultural understanding.

Similarly, we have remained uncertain as to the significance of the social presence of music. Annoyed at having social scientists condescendingly grant us the appeal of music as a *reflection* of social life, nevertheless we have stopped short of claiming it to be highly *constitutive* of culture and personality. In fact, it can be both, depending on a complex set of variables in given moments. One way people stitch their lives together is through musical memories, which act as milestones. Oliver Sacks (1987), a neurologist, describes an elderly patient who was nearly driven crazy by a set of hitherto-unremembered songs from her youth, which started running spontaneously and incessantly through her mind like an unstoppable, internal Walkman. This case study suggests the possibility that music serves as a soundtrack for our consciousness. In several other writings, including the most personal (*A Leg to Stand on* [1984], about his rehabilitation from a leg injury), Sacks cites music as a potential marshaling force for human action. In his latest case study featuring music, he is ever more emphatic: "Music, songs, seemed to bring Greg what, apparently, he lacked, to evoke in him a depth to which he otherwise had no access. . . . Music drew back the constraints of the disease . . . he no longer seemed to have a frontal lobe syndrome at such times, but was (so to speak) temporarily 'cured' by the music. Even his EEG, so slow and incoherent most of the time, became calm and rhythmical with the music" (Sacks 1992:59). Yet it might be only at certain critical junctures or in severely isolated cases like Greg's that the potential of music manifests itself so sharply. On a daily basis, it can be hindrance as much as help, annoyance or anodyne as much as comfort and consolation. While Sack's evidence only underlines music's claim on our attention, it does little to clarify how to theorize music beyond an immediate or local social or historical context. As far as neurology, the jury is not even out, for the case has not yet been heard; even Sacks can only describe, not explain, the power of music.

What often happens is that observers settle on one facet of music's diamondlike array of surfaces and reflections. Particularly nonspecialists can accept or dismiss whole chunks of musical experience by taking a theoretical curve around them as an obstacle, as José Limón (1991) does in his recent work on the Mexican-American dance hall. In an elegant essay, he positions himself vis-à-vis his illustrious predecessor in Chicano expressive culture studies, Americo Paredes, who wrote a seminal book (1958) on the heroic ballad of the Texas-Mexican borderland, the *corrido*:

If the *corrido* was the major signifier of the critical politics of Americo Paredes's heroic world, then I take the polka as that of my own world—the polka not so much as a musical form, but as dance. I opt for the dancing rather than the music because, as [Manuel] Peña has clearly suggested (1985:157–161), the music is increasingly more open to late capitalist and postmodern commodification, while, in my view, the dancing stands at some critical distance from the postmodern effect. (Limón 1991:130)

Here Limón summarily dismisses music as ideologically corrupt, in contrast to the continued purity of the dance tradition. Of course, he is separating the "commodified" band from the "noncommercial" dancers here, making the distinction on a purely social organizational plane. Yet he himself wonders, as Yeats did, how we can "tell the dancer from the dance," signaling a unity of sound and motion that should have led him to a comprehensive analysis of the entire event. What about the selling of alcohol, so indispensable to the story he spins about an evening at the Cielo Azul café, or the commodified costumes of the dancers, so important to the image they wish to project, and the fact that they have borrowed dance steps from the mainstream, presumably commodified, practice? The careful bracketing of just the affective interaction of dancers from the entire event seems to belie Limón's ethnographic stance.

Further, Limón's reading of Peña's pioneering description of the border dance-band world (of which more later) seems willful. Today's Mexican-American *conjunto* musicians are no more "commodified" in a "postmodern" way than most musicians in most places have been over the last century, since the advent of commercial sound recording and the subsequent technology-driven media. Further, do not the musicians themselves form a component of the community that merits a close, sympathetic look? In most such "ethnic" contexts, the men on the bandstand also have day jobs and belong to exactly the same world as the dancers, which is in itself an important reason for the success of their music in motivating the dance. Anyone who has seen Les Blank's film *Chulas Fronteras* (1975) is likely to carry away the image of the famed musician Narciso Jimenez on his daily rounds as a zookeeper. Limón's stance seems to distance the "pure" dancers from the "contaminated" musicians, an uncharacteristically romantic view from a hard-headed participant-observer who takes pains to empathize with, but not condescend to, his informants.

Even on a technical level, the relationship of dancers to the band (as detailed below) is too important to overlook. Yes, the band "choreographs" the dancers, but it is just *because* musicians are scrupulously careful to please the paying public that they create a joint aesthetic for which both must take responsibility—and credit, if the atmosphere is as positive as Limón suggests. Finally, seeing the Cielo Azul café as a totally distinctive place is certainly correct at one level—the Mexican-American experience is unique—but separating its pleasures and participants into mutually exclusive categories does not help us in the broader, comparative framework I seek to outline here. My own interests, detailed below, lead toward a general consideration of subcultural band-ing, suggesting some common features across in-group lines.

I do not mean to criticize an anthropologist who has taken his own vernacular expressive culture seriously. Limón is exactly the type of ally ethnomusicology needs as it reaches out to nonspecialists. There is simply a problem that arises when one narrows the focus too much, every bit as damaging as when one generalizes too glibly. The latter problem has recently been raised by Lila Abu-Lughod, an anthropologist who has done precise and elegant work in demonstrating the value of expressive culture studies. Her attack against generalization (Abu-Lughod 1991) grows from a strong interest in valorizing women's experience of a (Bedouin) society that the earlier literature viewed through too male a lens: by leaving out half the culture, the picture lacked depth. Yet in specifying the content of women's contribution in her insightful book *Veiled Sentiments*, (1986) Abu-Lughod, like Limón, limits her scope by overlooking the purely *musical* component of the sung verse creations that form the core of her research. Back on the Texas border, Americo Paredes, archaic though he might seem to Limón, at least provides the notation of *one* melody of the ballad his study is about before closing the book to music as a vital, indispensable part of performance. So, whether it is the figure of the musicians themselves or the expressive means by which Bedouin poetesses or Texas-Mexican border bards convey their craft, music, though appreciated, is still scanted.

Beyond the presence or absence of music within today's metadisciplinary explorations, a methodological issue implicit in the works just mentioned is this: in surveying a scene, what are the *units* of analysis and what are the *levels* on which one works? To a great extent, this twofold question occupies pride of place in the chapters to follow. In Limón's case, the possible units are the reflexive ethnographer, the dancers, the musicians, the club owner, the music/dance repertoire, the dress and codes of etiquette, the food and drink consumption, and so forth. The levels include the plane of performance itself, the construction of a typical evening's entertainments, the management of subcultural dance halls, the individual experiences and views of participants, the patterns of group interaction, the nature of gender relations, and even larger levels like *mexicano* culture. You might notice that units and levels are only sketches here—it is not always easy to tell them apart. My point is that no matter what the frame of reference, privileging some parameters is inevitable, but arbitrarily excluding any hardly helps us grasp the essence of a subculture. My own bias would of course lead me to argue for music as a primary component in contemporary societies, particularly in the microworlds that are the ethnographer's home.

Yet that home is increasingly under attack as a safe shelter for the researcher. As Abu-Lughod (1991:149) tells us, "Ideally there would be attention to the shifting groupings, identities and interactions within and across such borders as well. If ever there was a time when anthropologists could consider without too much violence at least some communities as isolated units, certainly the nature of global interactions in the present makes that now impossible." While here and below I applaud such sentiments, I think that we still need to look at small worlds as a way of being whole-earthers, to do "ethnographies of the particular," in Abu-Lughod's phrase. It is simply a matter of being ever more sensitive to context, both on the ground and in the head, which is in part what I take her title, "Writing against Culture," to mean. The nice thing about music is that it combines the local and the national, the immediate and the intercultural. By following the twists and turns of micromusics, by mapping the methodologies of this privileged form of expression, I hope to illuminate larger issues through smaller situations at a time when many of us are looking for ways to work. I do not think any simple analytical system will capture the pathos and the power of music in today's world of rapid deterritorialization and redrawing of boundaries, constant threat of terrorism or armed conflict, and simultaneity of marketing systems. Nor can I account for the diversity of local musical problems and solutions with the grand scheme of global cultural flow. I am simply trying to point out some general themes that might lead to a comparative approach.

I begin with a gesture toward "the Big Picture" of interlocked world sound systems that must serve as a backdrop today, then try to show how particular units and levels of analysis might mesh to form a temporary framework of inquiry within my chosen zone of Euro-America, all the while stressing the particular and sometimes peculiar ability of music to stand for a small group's self. I zoom in on musical strategies of subcultural life in the second part of the book, before closing with final reflections.

CHAPTER ONE

The Big Picture

❖

This is a book about micromusics, by which I mean the small units within big music cultures. They have not disappeared, despite the dismal forecasts of earlier commentators. If anything, they are proliferating today as part of a great resurgence of regional and national feeling and the rapid deterritorialization of large populations, particularly in the Euro-American sphere this book is about. The central fact is that today music is at the heart of individual, group, and national identity, from the personal to the political, from the refugee mother's lullaby to the "Star-Spangled Banner" at the baseball game. In reaching for comparative themes, I have tried to be very concise but also as inclusive as possible; I hope to have avoided being elliptical, though doubtless much of interest will be left out.

I shall proceed by both proposing and undercutting a set of terms as an exercise in defining a field of study that has seen many specialized contributions but little in the way of comparative thought. So let me first propose a trio of terms, all of which end with the same suffix: -culture. The hyphen stands for prefixes that modify that warhorse of a word *culture*, producing *subculture*, *superculture*, and *interculture*. Once it was easy to say that a "culture" was the sum of the lived experience and stored knowledge of a discrete population that differed from neighboring groups. Now it seems that there is no one experience and knowledge that unifies everyone within a defined "cultural" boundary, or if there is, not the total content of their lives. At least in the area these essays cover—North America and Europe/the former Soviet Union—at least for musical experience, people live at the intersection of three types of -cultures. English allows for a neat prefixing of such units, and my own style pushes me to use these nouns as temporary supports for a theory and method of current musical life that rests on a notion of overlaps, intersections, and nestings of the sort super-, sub-, and inter- represent.

Intuitively, I hope, super- suggests an overarching category, sub- an embedded unit, and inter- a crosscutting trend, and that's mostly what I mean. In lived experience, of course, people don't necessarily divide up their musical lives into such groupings, but often enough, when asked to articulate or to defend tastes or activities, people do in fact point to linkages, subordinations, import-export traffic, and other factors that implicitly support the notion of a -cultural musical life. The on-the-ground existence of numerous typologies, from the labels on record-store bins through the categories listed in ads for community music events and the names of courses offered in schools, suggests that people are quite aware of the varieties, values, and hierarchies of their musical -cultures. When a Cuban-American in a small New England city says to me, "This is a dead town; no music," he is acknowledging the presence of a mainstream to which he feels he does not belong as well as lamenting the lack of a music he craves. When the people who give the Grammy Awards create a category for "polka," they are commenting on the interaction between smaller and overarching music systems. When Greek-Americans invite a band from Greece rather than hire their own New York compatriots, they are putting their hard-earned money in service of a music culture that knows no nation-state boundaries. In thousands of such small-scale comments and decisions, everyday musicians and consumers create and sustain an extremely complex, highly articulated music system in the "late capitalist" and "emerging capitalist" societies of North America and Europe. The point of the following essays is to suggest some frameworks for thinking about, and for analyzing, that complexity. I do not mean to offer closed categories, but rather to stress the importance of overlapping and intersecting planes and perspectives. I have coined some new terms and used some old ones in new ways to refresh the intellectual palate, and I will not be free of my own paradoxes and contradictions.

Above all, *I do not mean to present a model, nor will I come up with one-sentence definitions of terms*. For me, terms are creatures of discourse, somewhere between stalking horses and red herrings. At best, the ones I offer here are what James Clifford calls "translation terms," each being "a word of apparently general application used for comparison in a strategic and contingent way." He warns us that "all such translation terms used in global comparison—words like culture, art, society, peasant, modernity, ethnography, I could go on—all such translation terms get us some distance *and* fall apart" (Clifford 1990:26). Like Clifford, what interests me is not a definition, but what goes on in your head when you match terms with reality.

By now it should be clear that much of my way of thinking overlaps current intellectual trends not much adopted yet (early 1992) in my discipline, ethnomusicology, most notably the British cultural studies tradition and its extensions and companions, such as postcolonial discourse, in the United States. For technical analysis, I have thought for many years that sociolinguistics offers those who study musical expression some acute insights. Of course, I will be unable to fill all the gaps in the current discourse on world music; my method is rather to make a number of proposals, sometimes in the form of schemes, typologies, headings. This does not mean that each gambit is self-sufficient, comprehensive, or final. I feel strongly that this approach mirrors not only our current understanding, but the data themselves. I hope simply that the following chapters will set off new chains of associations in the mind of a reader who will modify, elaborate, or even discard my proposals in a spirit of dialogue.

The present chapter proposes a broad overview of "the big picture," what Arjun Appadurai (1990) calls "the global cultural economy." It is followed by a dance around the three "-culture" terms in Part 2 (chapters 2, 3, and 4). In Part 3 (chapters 5 and 6) I watch the terms at work as they might apply to selected musical scenes in or near places I have worked or where I have located some relevant literature, some of which my students have produced. The coverage will be scattershot, since the available materials are scanty. I would simply have to wait too long for the necessary comprehensive survey work to be done for my perspectives still to be useful.

This book is not my first comparative venture; alongside my work on particular sociomusical contexts I have spun off a few more theoretical pieces on issues that I find absorbing (codeswitching in music; multilingualism as a global issue for music studies; the problem of "revival" movements), and some thoughts and perhaps paragraphs from those articles (Slobin 1979, 1983, 1986) reappear here in different dress; a shorter version of this volume appeared as Slobin 1992.

Like everyone else writing about the "multicultural" mosaic/stew/salad bowl/former melting pot we inhabit in Euro-America, I am acutely aware of the pitfalls of describing the musical experience of a variety of communities I neither grew up in nor have close working ties with. I can rely only on flexibility and a lack of dogmatism, not so much to bridge the gap between those who live the experience and those who analyze it, but to suggest that while group histories and social forces separate us, our personal expressive lives are inextricably tied to similar networks and patterns of possibilities, however unevenly and even inequitably they may be applied. Lucy Lippard (1990:21) has pointed out that "we have not yet developed a theory of multiplicity that is neither assimilative nor separative—one that is, above all, relational." My own attempt here is to be as relational as possible, to lay out the musical interplay—the cultural counterpoint—between individual, community, small group, state, and industry. It is a piece without a score for a collective without a conductor. I'm only working on the orchestration, the distribution of the many timbres and colors that are often stronger than the theme or the harmony, if either can be heard in this improvisation at century's end.

I've limited myself to Euro-America, including the former USSR as part of Gorbachev's "European home"; more time will have to pass before the Soviet successor states can be folded into the discussion. Ethnomusicology has been less attracted to this region than to Asia, Africa, and Latin America. Also, the supposedly "advanced" state of the region makes it in some ways a bellwether, or at least trend-setter, for other regions, in the evolution of new forms of capitalist democracy, the collapse of the socialist system, and the latest trends in self-definition of emerging nation-states. As mentioned earlier, I've been working on and traveling in Euro-America for some twenty years, after rounding off the first phase of my research life in Afghanistan/Central Asia (1967–72). Yet before localizing, I'll begin with the big picture, the overall context of world musical systems today, of which our Euro-American study is just one—if sometimes anomalous—case. Setting aside the "-cultures" approach for the moment, I plan a two-pronged grappling with the global. To begin with, I'll introduce what I find a most useful recent representation of worldwide culture patterns, Arjun Appadurai's "-scape" system, suggesting its musical implications, then introduce another perspective, centered on the term *visibility*, which comes at things from a different, yet overlapping plane of analysis.

Appadurai (1990) proposes viewing the "global cultural economy" in five dimensions, as a "set of landscapes," which he terms *ethnoscapes*, *mediascapes*, *technoscapes*, *finanscapes*, and *ideoscapes*. In a way, the handy suffix "-scape" is somewhat misleading here, since it implies a rather fixed perspective, whereas Appadurai regards his dimensions and the people who inhabit them as fluid, overlapping, and disjunctive. He feels that "the warp of stabilities is everywhere shot through with the woof of human motion" (7), and that "current global flows . . . occur in and through the growing disjunctures" between the five -scapes (11). It is a vision of a planet in flux, with a population that is creating "imagined worlds" based both on hard reality and on fantasy nourished by the shifting -scapes.

The -scapes themselves need fleshing out. *Ethnoscape* describes the viewpoint of "tourists, immigrants, refugees, exiles, guestworkers, and other moving groups and persons" rather than of the more traditional stable populations that ethnographers and economists use as standard units. This is because such moving groups are more visible and influential than they used to be, and even at home, "deterritorialization" of populations through economic, political, and cultural alienation means that everyone has an active ethnoscape these days. The other -scapes are similarly skewed. The *technoscape* features an "odd distribution of technologies," and a quirky movement of money produces an unsettled *finanscape*, so that "the global relationship between ethnoscapes, techno-scapes and finanscapes is deeply disjunctive and profoundly unpredictable, since each of these landscapes is subject to its own constraints and incentives . . . at the same time as each acts as a constraint and a parameter for movements in the others" (8). Meanwhile, there are deeply significant *mediascapes*, which, "whether produced by private or state interests, tend to be image-centered, narrative-based accounts of strips of reality" from which people make their own life-scripts (9). Finally, *ideoscapes* represent a different conceptual domain, derived from Euro-American Enlightenment thought and now unmoored throughout the world as floating images like "freedom, welfare, rights, sovereignty, representation and the master-term democracy" (10).

Appadurai's angle of vision is novel and refreshing. Seeing things globally is helpful, as is avoiding monolithic answers: there is no overall sense to the system, no hidden agency that controls the flow of culture. No one parameter is paramount—not populations, money, ideology, media, or technology—and each factor is only partly dependent on the other. Things are highly kinetic and extremely volatile, not only because of economics, but also because the "imagined world" (that popular term taken from Anderson 1983) of an individual or group is itself an actor on the world stage. This residue of personal and cultural difference is not clearly explained by Appadurai but is a major component of his scheme, for he continually appeals to the resistance to homogenization and an insistence on local understandings.

The implications of this worldscape for a view of music are worth considering for an ethnomusicology that is itself unmoored from older ideologies, adrift in the movement of technologies and media, and confused by constant deterritorialization of music-makers. If nothing else, it is helpful to think of music as yet another wild card in a game for which there are no known rules. To switch metaphors, music is woven into the cultural fabric Appadurai presents as one of the most scarlet of threads, created by ever-evolving technologies, transmitted by media, marketed through high and low finance, and expressive of private and public ideoscapes of autonomy and control for shifting populations. Even in the relatively middle-class worlds of the United States and Sweden, people polled cite music as one of the most satisfying components of their lives, and it may well have an even more profound connection to culture among the much less crystallized groups of greatly deterritorialized nations. Even the depersonalized, grand industrial systems take music very seriously. By tuning into music, we can hear the play of the -scapes.

Take the example of Pepsico's decision in March of 1989 to present Madonna's new video simultaneously across the world as part of a commercial. This event was itself preceded by a "softening-up" advertisement that showed an Australian Aboriginal trekking into an outback bar and watching the new release on television. The acknowledgment of music as the medium for a highly capitalized corporate moment is clear here. The attempt to create a unified media-, techno-, and finanscape is apparent, bringing to bear a seemingly unavoidable set of variables on the planet's population. Yet the ideoscape and ethnoscape deflected the thrust, decentered the momentum of this effort to control. The Madonna video in question was *Like a Prayer*, a baroque and bizarre play on Catholic, erotic, and postcolonial imagery, which demonstrated the singer's almost legendary drive to control her career and promote through provocation. The disjuncture between Pepsico's expectations and Madonna's presentation was disastrous: a fundamentalist Christian media watchdog threatened a product boycott, and Pepsico withdrew the commercial after only one showing in the United States. The corporate spokesperson denied that censorship was involved, saying the "consumers were confusing the message from the video with the message from the commercial, so 'why fuel that confusion? It was better to call it a day'" (Horovitz 1989).

The costs to Pepsico were high. The worldwide moment was billed as "the largest one-day media buy in history" (Applegate 1989), and Pepsico was forced to honor its five-million-dollar contract with Madonna, all the result of the musician's intransigence at letting Pepsico preview her video. This scenario already shows a sharp disjuncture between the corporate-controlled -scapes and Madonna's personal ideoscape. But even the most orthodox, mainstream ideoscape Pepsico might have picked for its message would have had no guarantee of commercial or cognitive success. For example, the very Australian Aboriginals Pepsico depicted as part of a target market are known to make the most diverse readings of mediated materials, particularly televised and musical programs, harvesting a bumper crop of sounds and images for their own pleasures and meanings.

Shift the kaleidoscope of -scapes and a different configuration defines the musical moment. Since Tanzania's topography does not allow for nationwide television broadcasting, in the 1980s the state provided video setups for towns, where collected viewers could watch approved programs (Krister Malm, conversation 1988). It would appear that the media-, ideo-, techno-, and finanscapes merge here, except that the nature of the video technoscape is somewhat anarchic. Viewers quickly discovered they could produce or smuggle in materials of their own choosing, to the government's dismay. In a conflict of imagined worlds, the local ethno- and ideoscapes won out, aided by low-cost financing and a flexible, self-controllable technology.

Implicit in Appadurai's framework and in the two examples just cited are questions of control and evasion that shine through the translucent interplay of cultural forces. I will return to this crucial question, usually summed up by the keyword *hegemony*, a bit later; at the moment, I want to propose a different scheme of relationship among global musics to provide a foil for Appadurai and another source for speculation.

Like traditional folksingers, today's music-makers tend not to care about the origins of items in their repertoire, domesticating a wide variety of sources to perform useful household tasks. The outcome of a long-planned multimillion-dollar advertising jingle is most often the enrichment of the schoolyard scene or a good tune for the shower. Omnivorous consumers, we take in any musical nourishment. To put our wide-ranging activities into some context, let me invent an analytical perspective based on the term *visibility*. Viewed from a particular vantage point, the world musicscape today consists of just three types of musics. By a *music*, I mean an easily recognizable style and practice complex of the sort that we label and describe in scholarship, that stores organize into bin headings, or that festivals use as criteria for inviting ensembles. Here, *visibility* means the quality of being known to an audience, and I suggest three types of visibility: local, regional, and transregional.

Local musics are known by certain small-scale bounded audiences, and only by them. This type of musical complex is what ethnomusicologists traditionally searched for high and low. When I first went to Afghanistan in 1967, I thought my mission was to locate, identify, and describe such local musics, and whenever I encountered musics of wider visibility, I was annoyed. For instance, I noticed that the existence of a national radio music interfered with these local styles, downgrading their status. At that time, it seemed there were many such local musics, a definitive collection of which would define our forthcoming map of the musical world. I was bolstered in this view by anthropology's belief in a numbered set of world cultures and by my own society's division of its population into "ethnic groups," each of which ought to have its own distinctive music. Such musics still exist. To take European examples, one can find them in valleys of Yugoslavia, in villages of the Russian North, or among Norwegian fiddlers. There are probably increasingly fewer of such musics, but they play a vital role as potential additions to the pool of musical resources available to broader audiences, to which I now turn.

Regional musics are less easy to define, since I am using the term *region* in an offbeat way. If *local* can be bounded by a village or valley, then *region*, intuitively, is a somewhat larger zone of contiguous territory. However, I have in mind a much more flexible sense of region, partly as a result of the spread of broadcasting and recordings. Of course, there are still classic regions, as in the understanding I have of, say, Slovenia or Slovakia. Widening the focus, Scandinavia sometimes creates a region, as when it is unified by an interest in the dance/tune form called *polska*. Or the German-speaking lands might form a region, if you look at the unified way four adjacent countries with different ideologies, politics, and local musics domesticated Anglo-American rock in the 1950s–1970s (Larkey 1989). I might even want to label Europe a region as a whole, if we look at the Eurovision Song Contest, so visible internally, yet invisible elsewhere in the world.

Regions also pop up in the linkages among diasporic communities, groups far from a perceived homeland and sharing a familiar music. In the United States, the Polish polka exists in a region of population pockets stretched across five thousand kilometers in widely separated urban areas. Within this regional music, there are traditional local styles: Chicago versus East Coast. The fact that the former began to dominate the latter shows a move from local to regional visibility. In this case, the regional diasporic music is isolated: American polka bands do not affect Poland. Yet the increasing mobility of emigré groups means that local musics feed into regional styles as isolated groups become part of a network. For example, the music of Puerto Ricans in Hawaii, which remained local for decades because of the great distance between diaspora and homeland, will now slide into regionalism. Much quicker regionalization is common, as when Turks arrive in Berlin or Stockholm and make immediate musical linkages to the homeland. So inhabitants of my musical regions can be nearby or far away, united as members of an imagined world of taste and practice, linked by face-to-face or electronic interaction, moving at a rate of slow or rapid style shifts.

Transregional musics have a very high energy that spills across regional boundaries, perhaps even becoming global. This category of musics is increasing rapidly due to the mediascape, which at any moment can push a music forward so that a large number of audiences can make the choice of domesticating it. There are older examples of this process, such as the opera or operetta aria, the waltz, the tango, the Neapolitan song; it needs only a transmitting medium of great carrying power, like sheet music or the 78 rpm sound recording. Some transregional musics are more unevenly distributed than others—compare Indian film songs with Anglo-American rock—and not all transregional scatter is accomplished by the media. For example, there is the highly influential genre of the protest song with guitar. In Sweden, I heard a Saami (Lapp) song from Norway directed against an intrusive hydroelectric project, written in Latin American style. These examples concur with Appadurai's findings: the assorted -scapes that channel the music are rather independently variable. The concatenation of media, financial, and technological power that gives commercial styles such transregional thrust is quite absent in the case of the protest song. There, the ideoscape of activism ("democracy," "sovereignty") and an ethnoscape of estrangement have proved their power in spreading a musical practice across all continents. Even a single item like "We Shall Overcome," never on a Top Forty list, pushed by no disc jockey and not available in video format, turns up anyway wherever people's imagined world conflicts with harsh reality.

Yet even where mediated musics predominate, locals can choose from a wide variety of transregional styles and subtly modulate their preferences, avoiding seemingly obvious ideoscape models like the leftist song. I have been told (E. Catani, conversation, 1988) that at the moment when Uruguay's rulers eased political controls, allowing the local youths to choose from the full range of transregional styles, they selected neither the global hit parade nor the political song, perhaps feeling that each was a trap, but rather put their cash and commitment into New Wave groups like Siouxsie and the Banshees.

The sophistication of audiences means that while visibility is the first filter for acceptance, knowledgeability might then select out only carefully chosen styles. Musics are important enough to evoke the most finely tuned of consumer sensitivities. Here the techno/media/finance investment pays off only for certain players, and in unanticipated ways. In a correlation of sensibilities, perhaps it was the vaguely nonconformist ideoscape of the British singers that invited the Uruguayan audience to share an imagined world that was neither in Montevideo nor in London. I will return below more than once to this kind of unpredictability of choice, which may be based as much on an aesthetic as on a presumed politico-econo-ideological pattern.

Isolating visibility as a factor in today's musicscape matches Appadurai's keen interest in principles of global flow. Viewed this way, world music looks like a fluid, interlocking set of styles, repertoires, and practices that can expand or contract across wide or narrow stretches of the landscape. It no longer appears to be a catalogue of bounded entities of single, solid historical and geographical origins, and the dynamics of visibility are just as shifting as the play of the -scapes. To flesh out the scope of visibility in music-cultural flow, it might just be possible to identify a few common processes. Shifts of profile are very common nowadays; some are self-generated, others just happen. A music can suddenly move beyond all its natural boundaries and take on a new existence, as if it has fallen into the fourth dimension.

The most glaring of recent examples must be the fate of the Bulgarian State Radio Women's Chorus. Available through all the -scapes to the Euro-American world for decades, this manufactured, postpeasant singing style lay dormant on record shelves until the late 1980s. Suddenly, an accidental concatenation of the sort increasingly present in the arbitrary play of global cultural forces foregrounded the style so thoroughly that by 1990 it was awarded a Grammy, the zenith of visibility in the commercial music world. The Bulgarian women went from local to transregional in no time flat. The disjuncture of -scapes is particularly prominent here, since the 1990 Western ideoscape of Eastern Europe as an ever-more democratic and free-market corner of the world completely contradicts the philosophy of the creators of the women's chorus: state control of the national heritage. Just as Bulgarians were turning their backs on this approach, the rock-pop community and Hollywood were embracing it. Sometimes the mediascape doesn't know what the ideoscape is up to. The difference between local and transregional consumption is very pronounced in this case, showing how varied planes of analysis need to be brought to bear on one and the same music. It is unlikely that the Grammy has caused Bulgarians to accept the old Women's Radio Chorus as the proud emblem of upward musical mobility.

At the other end of the spectrum, we find visibility shifting through self-conscious creation and promotion. Jocelyne Guilbault (1990) has detailed the rise of *zouk* music of Guadeloupe as just such an effort on the part of a small, local music culture. In her account, the sparkplug of the band Kassav deliberately set out to invent a local style that would attract more attention to an overlooked island, and he succeeded wildly. *Zouk* became a transregional success through manipulation of the elaborate media- and technoscapes available today and apparently because it tickled the ideoscape—or the aesthetic sensibilities, or both—of a broad audience of Caribbean, European, and African listeners. When this phenomenon registered back on the island, *zouk* became the basis for a new Guadeloupean cultural consciousness. At the moment, the more traditional local pop style, *gwoka*, recently featured in a *New York Times* Sunday travel section, is posed to become the next product to vault the local boundaries. Guilbault frames her study as a gauntlet flung down before economists, who tend to use the term *development* in limited ways; music, she finds, can be a form of development in the -scapes of Guadeloupe.

Between the Bulgarian and the Antillean situation lie dozens of examples of level-shifting. Many follow a path I call validation through visibility. This happens when a higher profile causes a local or regional population to reconsider its own traditions; the occasion for this moment is usually outside prompting. To return to the example of Afghanistan, where national radio damaged local musics through neglect, in the early 1970s a changed political landscape caused the government suddenly to begin broadcasting local musics (Uzbek, Turkmen, Baluchi, Pushai) hitherto ignored in the quest for regionalization of a synthetic popular style. Local audiences in the North, struck by hearing their musicians on the air for the first time, reevaluated performers they had overlooked for years. Until then, if they wanted to hear their own musics, they had to tune in to the versions of Central Asian sounds emanating from the neighboring Soviet republics. These musics were in the same general language/style complex but featured a different ideoscape and regional musical dialect.

As cassette recorders became available, people suddenly had an opportunity to record their own towns' musicians for private use, evading, but stimulated by, both the Afghan and Soviet broadcast systems. In this way nomads in winter quarters could enjoy their favorite players and styles, a fine example of the selective use of the available combination of technoscape, ethnoscape, and ideoscape. The point here is that the impetus came from outside but provoked an unexpected response. Whereas Kabul hoped for greater allegiance by providing local musics, it merely triggered greater alienation from Radio Afghanistan among those listeners who had the technical means to extend their enjoyment beyond the one hour a week that the capital allotted for ethnic styles. Again, a fragmented mediascape allows for a lot of mischief.

The old Soviet situation provides a huge range of intentional and unintentional shifting of visibility. Take one esoteric example: the impact of the Yakut jew's harp. Not well known even in the USSR, this Siberian style of complex melody-building on a simple instrument was widely broadcast by the state media. According to Alekseev (1988), other groups with their own jew's harp traditions were so impressed by the Yakut virtuoso sound that they began to reconsider the possibilities of local styles. Alekseev calls this the "resonance effect," which in my terms means that within a closed system, raising the visibility of one music might cause sympathetic vibrations—and internal change—in others. This result was probably not the intent of the original broadcasts, showing once more how culture flow occurs as much between the cracks as through the accepted channels.

In the foregoing, I have shown my respect for Appadurai's tentative analysis of global cultural flow as a stimulus for thinking about music. Sometimes lining up touchstone musical example yields a satisfying matchup, while at other times the limitations emerge. As Appadurai himself concedes, his system has its own cracks and disjunctures. For example, he is admittedly ambivalent about the relationship between the nation-state and global patterning, preferring to talk about deterritorialization and the decline of central authority rather than take on the precise interplay of state and populace. He is equally reticent to set out the dynamics of state and commercial forces in any given society. Yet any cultural analysis must take into account the existence of sharply bounded nation-state entities, multigroup and problematic as they may be. Certainly, until very recently, the huge Soviet test case would have produced little of value in terms of global cultural flow. Until 1990, the "East bloc" had its own subglobal circulation of culture, as did China and, to a lesser extent, India—nearly half the human race. Of course, the pressure of global flow tends to break down local resistance, but we must look to the inner network while keeping an eye on cross-state linkages.

Watching both sides of the road has become a central problem in ethnomusicology. Geared as we are to "socially situated" music "in context," or "in culture," we have made little of intersocietal connections. Such cross-boundary studies as we have (the foremost probably being Wallis and Malm's 1984 work on the phonogram industry) tend to focus on just one or two -scapes, finding it understandably hard to delineate the whole plane of interaction of diverse, complex, and shifting units of cultural analysis.

I have tried to accomplish two things in this opening exercise. The first of these is to draw attention to the issue of the global versus the local or, more properly, of the global within the local and vice-versa. For the remainder of this book I will stick to my chosen geographic domain, Euro-America. The second point I've tried to make is both how useful and how limiting it is to work through any particular conceptual grid, to view things from a given perspective. Both the "-scape" and "visibility" gambits are suggestive and perhaps even explanatory, up to a point, and at that point, you put on a different pair of glasses. I don't mean to belabor the optical metaphors that crowd current theoretical writing; maybe it's because I've worn bifocals for some years that I'm comfortable peering over, then under, to reconfigure my field of vision. Switching to computer glasses, as I do to write these lines, provides yet another version of depth of field, focal length, and perspective, all appropriate analogies for what happens when you start to write. Of course, I am not alone in noticing that to take account of current expressive culture, you need to match your vision to the multifaceted nature of the material. Surveying American multicultural visual arts, Lucy Lippard (1990:14) argues for "the negation of a single ideal in favor of a multiple viewpoint and the establishment of a flexible approach to both theory and practice." As for terminology, she points out that "the fact that there are no euphonious ways to describe today's cross-cultural exchange reflects the deep social and historical awkwardness underlying that exchange" (15). My own multiple viewpoint leads me now to turn to journey through an imaginary landscape of musical supercultures, subcultures, and intercultures.

PART TWO

❖

SETTING THE
TERMS

❖

CHAPTER TWO

The Superculture

❖

My notion of superculture has to do with the term *hegemony*, which will occasionally make an appearance in these essays. Like so many others these days, I have been deeply informed by this Gramscian term as amplified by Raymond Williams (1977). There are four main lessons I draw from Williams's commentary on Gramsci's rather sparse texts:

1. Societies (nation-state bounded regions) have an overarching, dominating—if not domineering—mainstream that is *internalized* in the consciousness of governments, industry, subcultures, and individuals as ideology. Let us call it hegemony.

2. Hegemony is not monolithic. There is no Board of Directors that monitors hegemony daily, adjusting and fine-tuning it. It can be formal and informal, explicit and implicit, conscious and unconscious, bureaucratic and industrial, central and local, historical and contemporary.

3. Hegemony is not uniform; it does not speak with one voice. It is complex, often contradictory, and perhaps paradoxical.

4. Hegemony is contrapuntal: there are alternative and oppositional voices in this cultural fugue that affect and shape the "themes." Points 3 and 4 mean that hegemony may be dissonant as often as harmonious, since no one knows the score.

As much as I admire this formulation, I find that making it operational means you run up against two unasked and unanswered questions: how do you know hegemony when you see it? If you find it, how do you apply it to a given component of culture, such as music? There are, in short, dangers here. An easy response to the first question might lead you to assume that almost anything is an example of hegemony, since there is no picture of it on the post office wall to compare with the suspect you've rounded up. Quick applications that avoid the second question can lead you to make facile generalizations (often seen in rock criticism) about the relationship of unexamined "dominant classes" or assumed ideologies to music-makers or consumers.

I offer no easy answers, only intuitions, the hunches of an ordinary citizen. *It seems* that if social forces compel American record producers to put warning labels on recordings of popular music, then a dominant ideology must be at work about both the power and the suitability of music. *It would appear* that if 95 percent of American record production is controlled by a handful of companies, then the relationship between this group and the remaining 5 percent must be unequal. *One can imagine* that if years of lobbying mean that a "polka" or "Hispanic" category is added to the Grammy awards of *"the* music industry" (note the definite article here), then some alternative musics have been seeking recognition, and that they *want* to be co-opted into a mainstream, the definition of which both sides have accepted. If Hispanic listeners in Hartford or New York complain that local Spanish-language stations don't play the music they want to hear, *you might think* that even within a subculture, the needs of commerce take priority over those of consumers. In short, I imagine that a commonsense approach, rather than a high-theoretical one, would help best in trying to see whether and how hegemony is embodied in the daily musical life of particular populations.

Yet the assumptions above are not fully warranted. The commonsense observer is just as permeated by the ideology as anyone else. Since ideology reflects hegemony, this sort of analysis represents hegemony commenting on itself. This prospect is frightening if you like observers to be "detached," less so if you see hegemony not as a plot, but as an everyday practice whose natives can be extremely articulate. At the extreme, there seems little difference between "hegemony" and "culture." It is exactly this problem of knowing where hegemony starts and stops that makes it so hard to use as an analytical tool. Its strength, I think, lies in the kernel of its claim: that there is unequal distribution of power within societies and that this distribution is both formulated and contested on a daily basis by everyone, in both deliberate and intuitive ways.

This broad, compelling insight has helped generate a variety of refreshing retreats from approaching culture with industrial-strength intellectual solvents that would strip the veneer of everyday life down to the hard structure beneath the surface. Instead, we find increasing interest in "multiform, resistant, tricky and stubborn procedures that elude discipline without being outside the field in which [they are] exercised, and which should lead us to a theory of everyday practices" (de Certeau 1984:96). Perhaps beginning with Erving Goffman, the "everyday" has become the preferred plane of analysis: the arena of daily life as the showcase and battleground of hegemony. As a legacy of early modernist analysis of city life (the Baudelaire-to-Benjamin line), the streets become central to works like de Certeau's "Walking in the City" (1984), with an approach that can now be found even among cultural geographers, as in Pred's (1990) astute analysis of the spatial quality of turn-of-the-century working-class cultural resistance in Stockholm. Following paths broken by Barthes, cultural theorists also seek out the mundane haunts of the beach or the video arcade (Fiske 1989). Unlike earlier analysts of power relations in modern culture, from Foucault's prisons to Mills's power elite, today's writers prefer shopping malls to the halls of Congress, bathrooms to boardrooms. Even when observers focus on cultural construction teams (Gitlin 1983, Faulkner 1983), they tend to present the producing clique as a bunch of regular citizens who, thrust into a power position, try to psych out the everyday consumer or simply repeat successful formulas—no maniacal plotters of hegemonic control here.

Let me now introduce my word *superculture*. Unlike *subculture* and *interculture*, I have rarely seen it used elsewhere, even though it seems a logical companion. Available terms like *collective mode of administration*, *dominating classes*, even *mainstream*, seem unwieldy, simultaneously too specific and too vague. If hegemony is complex and contradictory, no single "dominant formation" can account for its action. A truly nebulous term like *superculture* does the job better for my purposes. It implies an umbrellalike, overarching structure that could be present anywhere in the system—ideology or practice, concept or performance. The usual, the accepted, the statistically lopsided, the commercially successful, the statutory, the regulated, the most visible: these all belong to the superculture.

In terms of music, the superculture would include at least three basic components:

1. An industry, including its alliances with techno-, media-, and finanscapes, consummated through the ceremony of advertising, justifying the ways of the superculture to man, woman, and child. The emergence of a *music* industry is surely one of the triumphs of capitalism, channeling the prerogatives of church, court, nation, and home through the energy of the talented individual, now raised to commodity. This harnessing of the unbounded spirit of music keeps tightening as packagers and distributors gain experience in the subtle techniques of co-optation and market penetration, most flamboyantly deployed in the United States. The easy way we accept the notion of Christian rock or ultra-Orthodox Jewish pop, commercialized spirituality at work, shows how

well hegemonic principles can diffuse throughout societies. The internal expressive policing of subcultures through systems like the "Hispanic" market's cable networks does more to draw its subjects into the superculture than do the public schools and the police. Boycotts against Univision for a television columnist's interpretation of Puerto Rican life and a reluctance to buy the *Miami Herald*'s Spanish-language edition because of its politics (*New York Times*, October 15, 1990) tell us just how much subcultures care about outside control.

Yet rarely is music, the silent socializer, the focus of protest against hegemony. You simply have to try to ignore Julio Iglesias if he doesn't represent your particular musical roots—although he slips into your consciousness anyway. Like it or not, you end up having to identify with his success, as defined through sales figures and official recognition (for example a Grammy Award), terms of achievement that the superculture invents, then celebrates through the celebrity cult. Every Finnish- or Serbian-American knows the pantheon of commercially sanctioned winners the group has produced. Often the state acts as godfather to these children of the marketplace: in 1990, Congress appropriated half a million dollars to turn the boyhood home of the mainstream bandleader Lawrence Welk into a landmark. The idea was to create a pilgrimage point for German-American culture in a "culturally depressed" area, generating tourist income by glorifying one man's skill at leaving his expressive heritage behind to achieve superculture success. Another hand-in-glove enterprise is the incursion of the National Academy of Recording Arts and Sciences (which invented the Grammy Awards) into the classroom as part of a "Grammy in the Schools" project, explicitly meant to nurture an audience for NARAS members' commercial productions. This interplay of government and industry leads us to the second domain of the superculture:

2. The state and its institutionalized rules and venues. Governments have many tentacles for reaching deep into the citizen's musical life. Indoctrination begins in primary school, but we have no serious studies of the content of music books across time and space to sense what long-term strategies the state uses in its mandated hours of musical enculturation. We can guess that long-term immersion in nationalist and nostalgic songs leaves its traces. We know that in America, just as child-targeted television prepares little minds to be consumers, so school music-making draws steadily on merchandized materials to form the consciousness of citizens. In the United States, even the national classics—the songs of Stephen Foster—were commercially composed, the gap between the schoolroom and the marketplace being exceptionally

small. A glance at magazines for high school bands reveals an extraordinary commodification of team spirit, exalted through a thousand local parades, product endorsements, and television exposure of high school and college football bands; where the state leaves off and commodification begins is almost impossible to tell, as already noted for the Grammy project.

This activity affects subcultures in two ways: through erasure and through stereotypes. Erasure is implicit in the unsung melodies of a hundred micromusics, missing from the classrooms of Euro-America. Like the lack of one's language, the absence of familiar music sends a clear supercultural signal to children. Stereotypes blossom everywhere, often as a part of officially sponsored cultural pluralism. American school music books, have tended to include songs from a variety of "homelands," each item brand-naming whatever subculture is depicted.

Outside the schoolhouse, governments everywhere control music through regulation, a separate topic too large to handle here. Let me just point out some implications for subcultures. In the old Eastern bloc, official state regulation and erasure systems alternated with attempts to co-opt unofficial culture, as witnessed by, say, the ups and downs of jazz in the USSR (Starr 1980) or rock in Bulgaria (Ryback 1990). In Western Europe, attempts to shut down pirate radio have yielded to opening the skies to cable companies, a shift toward the American model, yet state manipulation continues at various levels of regulation. In a patchwork system like Yugoslavia's, until very recently one could find independent, regional record producers that nevertheless had to turn to the state (which took a share of profits) to press their records (Ljerka Vidić, conversation, 1988). Or a local government sometimes decided to tax officially nonvalued commercial musics to foster more acceptable styles (Radmila Petrović, conversation, 1984)). In the United States, for years Congress was stymied in trying to regulate digital audio tape by not knowing whether to side with the producers of playback equipment (who favored it) or with producers of sound recordings (who opposed it). Examples abound of this cozy yet complex interaction of state and industry. The government probably bows to the demands of commerce more often in America than in Europe.

Nowhere are the cracks and disjunctures of hegemony more apparent than at the margins of the public and private, where contradictory values are laid bare. In the United States, the dialectic between community control of obscenity and free-speech rights is foregrounded or backgrounded in a cyclical fashion (it leaped to the forefront again around 1990). Levels of government, ranging from town councils to the Supreme Court, may disagree, and branches of government, including Congress, the courts, and agencies of the executive, may disagree. Indeed, these agencies may even work at cross purposes when it comes to enforcing vaguely worded statutes on matters like licensing, royalties, and copyright. Despite the strains in this intrasuperculture alliance of state and commerce, the tendency to paper over the cracks is very strong. In 1989, when local governments began prosecuting allegedly obscene art, records, and even posters advertising records, the music industry's response was defensive in terms of profits, not rights. Warning labels were slapped on recordings and internal monitoring of lyrics and artwork intensified. Spokespeople assured interviewers that this was not self-censorship, just sound business. Lawrence Kenswil, of MCA Records, stated: "A record company has the right to decide which records to put out. It's just a matter of where you draw the line. That's not censorship. Censorship is when someone *else* tells you" (quoted in Browne 1990).

A particularly insightful recent case of hegemonic crosstalk comes from Ice-T's 1992 album *Body Count*, which contained the controversial song "Cop Killer." Across the United States, policemen's organizations began a boycott of Time-Warner, the record label's parent company. However, African-American police organizations refused to join the ban-the-song movement, and The National Black Police Association declared that Ice-T "is entitled to voice his anger and frustration with the conditions facing oppressed people." (quoted in Pareles 1992). Pop music critic Jon Pareles notes the complexity of the question of democratic opposition to the superculture, when initiated by one sub-branch of the superculture itself: "the police aren't just any pressure group; on or off duty, they belong to the armed force of the state." Meanwhile, the artist himself wondered aloud why the white actor Arnold Schwarzenegger could portray a ferocious, mechanical cop-killer on screen (*Terminator* 2), while a black songwriter is not allowed to voice the imagined homicide of an African-American fictional character. It appears that supercultural power is brought to bear on unsettling topics and targets selectively, and that subcultures feel more of the brunt of efforts at control.

It is ironic that precisely at this juncture, Eastern European governments were loosening their hold on subcultural strivings and learning the value of co-optation. The great age of self-censorship there, so well described for decades (see Haraszti 1987 for a classic statement), has passed over into American practice. This interchange of methods of control only demonstrates the greater interdependence of the Euro-

American world. Equally unremarkable is the fact that each side chooses to ignore the lesson already learned by the other. Kenswil of MCA Records has probably not read Haraszti, while the emerging entrepreneurs of the old East are only slowly becoming aware of the painful complexities of balancing supercultural control with private creativity.

3. Less flagrant but more insidious strands of hegemony. These are the quiet agents of ideology that define the everyday, circumscribe the expressive. There is a huge body of shared assumptions about every aspect of music-making. Stereotypes and career paths for professional musicians are quietly enforced. For example, a friend of mine who applied for insurance was advised by his agent to put down "teacher" instead of "musician" as a profession—and he does not even look like a "minority" person, for whom the tag would have been double trouble. Performance contexts and their evaluation are tightly defined, particularly for micromusics that need defending or, at least, public explanation, for their very appearance, most commonly at officially sanctioned events celebrating "diversity." Last, but hardly least, the superculture provides a set of standardized styles, repertoires, and performance practices that anyone can recognize, if not like, a common coin of the musical national currency that we all carry around every day.

Like any other hegemonic subsystem, music spreads to subcultures and individuals through various channels, often overlapping, sometimes conflicting. In classic state-controlled systems like pre-1990 Eastern Europe/USSR, official and unofficial culture act like parallel tracks, with musical categories often jumping from one to the other. In Western Europe, state and commercial sources also offer a two-tier, interlocked system, while in the United States, it is primarily the multitentacled commodified culture that provides diversity and some dissonance. Just as cereal companies provide both heavily processed and "natural" products, with intermediate options, so changing and even hostile packagings like "soul," "country," "metal," or "rap" offer variety through commerce. A modest national consensus occurs when the national anthem is sung at sporting events, when a handful of standard Christmas songs streams relentlessly into every public space for several weeks at year's end, or when a commercial jingle penetrates the consciousness of children of all subcultures (for whom it is the major musical repertoire).

As always, the anomalous cases help clarify the main issues, and it is in that context that I would like to mention the former Yugoslavia, more specifically, the kind of music officially called "newly composed folk music" (henceforth NCFM), currently being studied by Ljerka Vidić in a dissertation in progress. NCFM is a folk-based style that

emerged from post–World War II urbanization. It rose to great promi-
nence in the 1970s and 1980s, becoming, from the point of view of sales,
a "popular" music of great power. Its institutional framework is complex, consisting of state superculture components like radio and television stations and the official press. Given Yugoslavia's socioeconomic
structure through 1990, however, there is an equally lively industrial
side to NCFM: record companies and unofficial press. These institutions are seemingly still under state control, but, as Vidić (letter, 1991)
says, "the fact that all of these institutions are government-founded is
of little help in understanding how they actually work or what kind of
music policy (if any) they apply." Although record companies are supposed to be institutions of "special cultural importance," they are not
government-subsidized. So while they fulfill the state command to produce tax-exempt classical and village music, they survive on the basis of
a commercial market they create and manage. As a result, the authorities have no control over NCFM. According to Vidić, "what seems to
be the major concern of those involved in the music industry is the *lack*
of controls over it." Meanwhile, the music itself "has from its inception
both blurred and emphasized the boundaries between regional, ethnic,
national, and foreign elements"; it now faces the new challenge of adapting to the greater assertiveness—indeed, the triumph—of regional over
national identity in Yugoslavia. "If record companies turn to their ethnically 'pure' audiences within the confines of their respective regions,
NCFM could be, for the first time, in the service of state regimes," says
Vidic. In other words, now that the Croatians are busily compiling a
dictionary that will remove the first part of the name of the hyphenated
(Serbo-Croatian) national language, official reshaping, or at least altered
patronage, of the musical vocabulary cannot be far behind.

Appadurai's -scapes seem to work well here in three ways. First, there
is a great deal of slippage between the components of hegemony, since
the articulation among techno-, media-, and finanscapes lacks precise
definition. Second, the ideoscape as a reshaping of imagined worlds
holds the "swing vote" in the allocation and understanding of how resources will be used. Finally, the volatility of the ethnoscape (through
urbanization and probably also emigration for work) plays an important role in keeping the cultural flow lively. There seems little room for
a cozy superculture partnership between state and industry in a society that never quite worked out their relationship and is now busily
renegotiating even that reasonably stable balance.

The foregoing is just a sketch of some main features of the musical superculture. My main concern lies not with an analysis of the

inner workings of hegemony but rather with the interplay of superculture and subculture, and extensions to the interculture, detailed below. Yet another important issue to be deferred is the relationship of individual music-makers/consumers to larger social units, what de Certeau (1984:96) and others call somewhat stiffly "a contradiction between the collective mode of administration and an individual mode of reappropriation." As I shall argue below, this leaves a space, indeed a cavernous hole, between the collective and the singular, where the subculture and its own subdivisions might be located. To bridge some obvious conceptual gaps, I need to turn now toward the subculture, the affinity group, the small-scale network of human bonding that fills in much of this theoretically troubling and socially contested space.

CHAPTER THREE

Searching for the Subculture

❖

When we look at micromusics, what units do we choose or, less clini-
cally, which voices do we listen to? In addition to the individual, there
are micro-units like the family, the neighborhood, the voluntary association, the festival organizing committee, the church board, and many
others that we tend to lump together when describing "the group."
Recent ethnic studies have begun to grapple with this issue. For example, Keefe and Padilla (1987), tackling the large topic of "Chicano
ethnicity," do so as an anthropologist-and-psychologist team precisely
because they feel that looking at either the individual or the group fails
to provide enough perspective, and that sociologists' overviews cannot
stand alone. This approach leads them to consider how both qualitative
and quantitative methods need to be used and how intragroup differentiation at the smallest level of family life is crucially important to
understanding the life of a subculture, and to stress the shaping nature
of small-scale networks. Similarly, Waters (1990) opens her work on
"ethnic options" by explaining how the confused nature of the all-too-
detailed 1980 U.S. census reports led her to move toward qualitative
work in targeted communities to sort out the situation. In cross-cultural
music research, Wallis and Malm's (1984) landmark work on the recording industry also begins with a statement about life beyond statistics,
with a strong stress on the importance of key individuals to marketing innovations and trends. All these caveats and suggestions resonate
with some of my current feelings about how music-making needs to be
studied.

To my mind, a partial groundwork for meaningful methodologies
was laid by Georg Simmel back in 1922, in his *Die Kreuzung Sozialer
Kreise*, rather awkwardly translated as "The Web of Group-Affiliations"
(Simmel 1955). He was probably reacting against a sociological ten-

dency to view the hectic search for meaning in urban environments as wholly negative, choosing instead to see the relationship between individuals and their choice of affiliations as constructive and positive: "from the combination [of chosen groups] he gains his maximum of individuality—the one group offering him opportunities for socialization, the other opportunities for competition." (156) Or, more strongly, "opportunities for individualization proliferate into infinity also because the same person can occupy positions of different rank in the various groups to which he belongs" (151). All of this "compensates for that isolation of the personality which develops out of breaking away from the narrow confines of earlier circumstances" (163), a reference to the set, almost ascribed roles in "tightly-knit primary groups" such as families, workgroups, or subcultures. Following out this approach, Simmel baldly states: "Thus one can say that society arises from the individual and that the individual arises out of association." As for the individual, "he is determined sociologically in the sense that the groups 'intersect' in his person by virtue of his affiliation with them" (150).

While not swallowing this whole, I find very useful in Simmel's formulation a perspective that sees just how complex and meaningful the interplay of personal choice and group activity can be both to individuals and to society. From the point of view of music studies, it is easy to blur the lines between single activists and whole traditions, between ensembles and institutions, and that blurring is understandable, given the kind of data our methods turn up. We interview musicians as star cultural performers, look at bands as small groups carrying styles, and tend to jump from these microworlds to the "group" as a whole. The problem crops up in surveying other expressive forms as well, as in Lucy Lippard's otherwise admirable book *Mixed Blessings* (1990), one of the few works to consider the problems of the new art arising from what she calls "a multicultural America." Throughout, she moves from consideration of individual artists producing singular objects to more general statements about the groups these artists might belong to or represent. For example, she states that "the art reproduced here demonstrates the ways in which *cultures* see themselves and others," then follows with remarks about choosing "younger and/or lesser-known *artists*" (Lippard 1990:4; italics mine), but fails to make explicit the linkage between *cultures* and *artists*. Yet I find that the ways in which individual music-makers stand for, influence, are accepted or rejected by larger social groupings—subcultures?—to be one of the most profoundly challenging issues of analysis.

In ethnomusicology, we might take a close look at the pioneering anthology on Euro-American musics that James Porter edited in 1978. One essay concentrates on a single fiddle tune (Burman-Hall), another on European connections of Cajun music based on historical principles (Marcel-Dubois), a third takes a more ethnographic look at a couple of individual Hungarian-American singers to make the same connections (Erdely), a fourth focuses in on the ideology of song composition in a sub-subculture (Koskoff on Hasidim), while a fifth moves out from a genre study to suggest ideologies based on waves of immigration (Forry on Serbian-Americans). As a set, this anthology admirably shows off the variety of possible methodologies in an embryonic field of study, and we cannot expect short articles to cover too much ground. Nevertheless, the overall format presents an almost bewildering mixture of levels and planes of analysis, leaving the reader to find some general vantage point from which to survey the whole landscape.

A closer look at a single essay in the 1978 volume may show what I mean. Christina Niles's very informative essay on the "revival" of the Latvian *kokle* zither showcases the powerful role of two key individuals, one who adapted the instrument to American use and one who produced an instructional manual that facilitated group organization. This primary narrative is overlaid with a description of three types of music-makers in the community: rank amateurs, talented amateurs, and elite specialists, all three of whom interact with the newly emerging *kokle*. Niles introduces a third theme, of waves of immigration; a fourth, relationship to the homeland; a fifth, superculture/subculture interplay in creating an ideology around zither ensembles; and a sixth, parent-child relations. She also briefly suggests a seventh theme, regional differentiation of musical scenes in America.

The hard part of this type of conscientiously thorough study is to put the pieces together convincingly. The strategy adopted here is to foreground one issue—the usefulness of *kokle*-playing as "a fashionable aspect of a more general 'back-to-tradition' movement among Latvian youth" (Niles 1978:00)—while throwing in as many other insights as one can manage. This strategy means that many issues of equal importance remain far in the background, while the highlighted topic of "identity" is shortchanged as well. As sensitive as this laying out of the complexity of a subculture's inner expressive life may be, it can present only some of the parameters and will find it hard to place the shifting circumstantial evidence in an integrated framework, since we have no general theory for the dynamics of subcultural life, just a set of rule-of-thumb possibilities. When is the pull of "Americanization" stronger than an interest in "revival" in Niles's formulation and why for a particular generation? Why is the moment ripe for the work of a couple of isolated activists to spread like wildfire through a subculture? When are generational concerns more important than family orientation or personal choice?

Niles attempts a quantitative approach to the last issue by interviewing fifteen students of two different age groups in one city, hardly a sociologist's dream sample, but as good as one usually gets in ethnomusicological studies. Conjectures are common—she argues, for example, that "rehearsals, concerts, and the annual kokle and folksong festivals are strong incentives for learning to play the instrument" but there is no backup data here. Evidence from both ethnic and non-ethnic ensembles might suggest that for young people, social conviviality and age-grade cohesion might be just as important (see Pearce 1984 on drum corps in the Connecticut Valley, Godmilow 1976 on members of the Chicago Serbian community). I am not specifically faulting Niles here; I find in my own studies the same problem of welding the disparate strips of observation into a finished work of analysis. I am proposing simply that the problem lies not in the incompleteness of the ethnography but in the lack of a unified model for subcultural expressive culture.

But even if such a model were developed, I would be highly suspicious of its explanatory power. If we take a wider view, "Latvianness" here can stand in for many such musical situations where focusing on "ethnicity" is part of the aim. Usually left untouched is Simmel's point that individuals have multiple identities and exist in a "web of affiliations." Latvian-American kid-*koklists* may also play in rock groups and marching bands; Latvian-American adults may belong to barbershop quartet circles. To take a European example, in an area of Sweden (Dalarna) considered the musical/folkloristic heartland of the country, the teenagers cruise the streets in 1950s American style, complete with old cars and rock 'n' roll personae, then shoulder fiddles on Sundays to play in family and local "folk" events (Ronström, conversation, 1990). This situation is not just an issue of superculture-subculture relations, or intercultural interference, but part of a simple Simmelesque observation: "The modern type of group-formation makes it possible for the isolated individual to become a member in whatever number of groups he chooses. Many consequences resulted from this" (Simmel 1955:140).

I cannot go fully into all those consequences here, nor do I think Simmel himself does much more than sketch out the main lines of the problem of the interplay of "isolated individuals," "group affiliations," and the larger society. However, we do now have a consistent and comprehensive model based on a single, small urban area that addresses the issue of levels of analysis: Ruth Finnegan's very substantive 1989 account of the English town of Milton Keynes. Finnegan was struck by the strong overlaps between local musical groups and national networks, family music-making patterns and institutionally based support systems (school, church). She tried to make sense of fragmentation by appealing to the notion of the musical "pathway." Finnegan was drawn to the term because anything else sounded too self-enclosed: "world" (from Becker 1982), "group," "community"—all had a limiting quality she found absent in the freewheeling cultural space of Milton Keynes, where "the musical worlds thus to some extent interpenetrated one another. Their boundaries were shiftable—and were shifted—by their participants" (Finnegan 1989:181.)

There is little comfort in the term, however, since it does not explain, but merely describes, the problem:

There seems, then, to be no single answer to why particular people find themselves on one or another of the established musical pathways . . . musical paths are voluntary . . . but to this awareness of free choice must also be added the patterns and constraints and opportunities that . . . help to draw individuals towards or away from particular paths . . . chief among these the influences of gender, of age, of stage in the life-cycle, the link to various other social groupings and . . . family musical background. (Finnegan 1989:317)

In short, Euro-American societies allow considerable leeway for choice along the lines of voluntarism, but within a grid of limitations that no one can change, indeed, that no one even thinks about. It is almost as if the many musical affiliations of Milton Keynesians were so many political parties in a multiparty liberal democracy, all of which were sworn to uphold the constitution, and as if voting were a function of family orientation, gender, age, ties to various other social groupings, and so forth. Of course, music provides ever so much more variety and satisfaction than politics; yet the overall relationship of personal choice to fixed givens might be comparable.

My reason for this probably overstated analogy is Finnegan's admission that versatility and flexibility are rather circumscribed culturally: "The established pathways were in a sense already there, as a route at least to begin on; they were part of the existing cultural forms rather than something that had to be calculated afresh each time" (ibid.:307). In fact, there is a great deal of control at all levels of her system. Some pathways are mostly in the hands of state bureaucracies, notably "classical" music, which is based on "progressive admission through recognized grades, guarded by specialist teachers and examiners" (134). Others, like church music, have a "dominant ideology" of "a close link between music and religion," so involve deeply rooted institutional support (221). These ideologically driven patronage systems mesh with the commercial motivation of entrepreneurs like pub-owners, who "wanted to encourage more women and saw music as one way of achieving this" (232). The hidden hand of the superculture is evident throughout the extraordinarily rich musical life of Milton Keynes, so English in its choice of musics yet so much a part of the Euro-American mainstream. Were we to take the superculture's side, we would cheer on Finnegan's description of the power of music to define social moments: "Music and musicians are thus recognized as having the special role of creating a space in social life and framing events as 'rituals'" (336). We would also applaud the way music organizes people's lives by offering both transcendence and orderliness: "Musical enactment is at once a symbol of something outside and above the usual routines of ordinary life and at the same time a continuing thread of habitual action running in and through the lives of its many local practitioners" (339).

Nothing Finnegan says hints at so much as a gram of the oppositional in every kilo of co-optation. Even rock turns out to be nonconfrontational, its accepted image as youth or working-class protest not being supported by her empirical data: "Perhaps the most prominent single characteristic . . . was a stress on individuality and artistic creation which accords ill with the mass theorists' delineation of popular music" (129). All of Finnegan's people end up feeling the same way about music, expressing "an unspoken but shared assumption . . . that there was something . . . unparalleled in quality and in kind about music which was not to be found in other activities of work or of play" (332). Ultimately, music in Milton Keynes seems to function at two levels: as a kind of socially patterned mode of self-fulfillment and as a regular, satisfying exercise in Victor Turner's *communitas*, a socially sanctioned feeling of oneness that both affirms and erases everyday boundaries. This account explains the problem of level-switching in analysis: are we looking at the personal or the social side of this somehow nondichotomous yet binary situation? Music seems to have an odd quality that even passionate activities like gardening or dog-raising lack: the simultaneous projecting and dissolving of the self in *performance*. Individual, family, gender, age, supercultural givens, and other factors hover around the musical space but can penetrate only very partially the moment of enactment of musical fellowship. Visible to the observer, these constraints remain unseen by the musicians, who are instead working out a shared vision that involves both the assertion of pride, even ambition, and the simultaneous disappearance of the ego.

This dilemma foils our analytical radar when we look at the structure of performance itself for social clues. They are abundant, ranging from physical grouping of performers through a hundred details of dress, leadership roles, and the ideology implicit in the aesthetic ideals of sound production, and have been mined by researchers ever since "performance" moved to the forefront in 1970s folklore and ethnomusicology studies. Yet performance is no more than a different perspective on the same issues. It tracks the social life into the pub and hall, but often does little to bridge the gap between the individual and the society, since while outsiders look for standard patterns, insiders may stress the rather ineffable notion of "musicality." According to Finnegan (307), "the achieved rather than ascribed nature of musical competence was one major theme in local music activity, when what you achieved musically was more important than who you were."

This observation brings us into the realm of the aesthetic, and only rarely do studies of Euro-American micromusics show how *aesthetic* rather than organizational/contextual aspects of performance betray a continuity between the social, the group, and the individual. One analytical moment of this sort can be found in Averill's (1990) work on American "barbershop" singing groups, where the singers' explicit notion of a "harmonic highway" which involves a satisfying return to "home" as part of an aesthetic complex that includes other elements such as the dominant subject matter of song texts. This aesthetic might then be linked, as part of an overall analysis, to the social situation of the ensemble as a whole. Such an approach is not surprising—indeed, it is even normal—in our view of African music-making, yet it is alien to the Euro-American context, where the notion of an everyday aesthetic has been very late in being recognized. No doubt the ideology of how to study the Other versus Ourselves has something to do with this imbalance.

Before turning back to this issue of "an overall analysis," let me tackle a single parameter to show the methodological tangle that arises in trying to comb out any one strand of a micromusic. I will use class for purposes of demonstration. The cultural studies background to my approach politely but firmly suggests that class be foregrounded. Yet class is highly elusive when we get down to cases. Finnegan (1989:329) flatly asserts that "in the Milton Keynes study the concept of class turned out not to be of particular significance either for participants' own perceptions or for any overall analysis of local musical practice." The situation is further complicated by early cultural studies problems in trying to map class onto music for subcultures. Briefly put, "style" features like clothing and music were seen as emblems of identity in youth subculture, a spin-off of a necessary "parent class," here the working-class (Hall and Jefferson 1975, Hebdige 1979). By 1981, Clarke pointed out the reductive nature of this approach, which tended to essentialize all subcultural group members and freeze the meaning of trends and styles. More recent British formulations take account of the considerable complexity of class in today's societies; a good starting point is Paul Gilroy's (1987:35) trenchant remark that "class today is a contingent and necessarily indeterminate affair." Gilroy's concern is with distinguishing class analysis from issues of race in Britain, a good example of how "contingent" things can get: "'race' can no longer be reduced to an effect of the economic antagonisms arising from production, and class must be understood in terms qualified by the vitality of struggles articulated through 'race.'" Moreover, such issues are not confined to Britain. Surely the relationship of class to something like race is of enormous importance in a country like France today, and always has been in the United States. That example is but one illustration of how hard it is to isolate class as a separable component.

In trying to sort out the relationship between micromusics and class, another phrase of Gilroy's might come in handy: "classes are only *potentially* constituted" (1987:31). In our terms, we might be able to identify a nice clean homology between music and class within a subcultural setting, as in Bourdieu's (1984) charts, where musical taste can be elegantly aligned with a variety of finely detailed class formations, or in Peña's (1985) very articulate account of Texas-Mexican listening habits, which show that different clusters of ensemble/genre/style can be class-contested. These seem to be cases where the potential for class expression through music has been realized. However, what often happens is that particularly in popular music studies, outsiders make conclusions about the class-related nature of a particular style, genre, or performer, despite the fact that, as Richard Middleton (1990:8) has pointed out, "particular cultural forms and practices cannot be attached mechanically or even paradigmatically to particular classes."

Charles Keil's interest in the polka as a "working-class" phenomenon might be one micromusical scene to investigate more closely. Keil (1982, Keil and Keil 1984) feels that the polka, spread across many American subcultures from midwestern Euro-Americans to southwestern Native Americans, defines a proletarian praxis. Yet it is a bit of a leap from the empirical observation that many Central/Eastern European urban communities share polka magic to the conclusion that this preference is class-related behavior. Virtually all of these groups suggest, sometimes explicitly, that country-western music is their point of class orientation, even to the extent of shaping their "ethnic" polkas. A Connecticut musician, describing the interaction of the genres, says: "We do a couple songs . . . which are country songs. . . . But you can turn them around into a polka . . . they're for your old country people and not just for somebody living in a big house. And that's what most real polka people are. They're common people; they're not rich people" (Spalding 1986:75).

McHale (1981) feels the same about the adoption of country music by the musicians she talked to in Franco-American Vermont, and Leary (1987:212) confirms the situation for another group of Euro-Americans, in the Midwest: "Such later forms as 'honky tonk' or 'hard country,' with its emphasis on the ruralite adrift in the city, were especially appealing to displaced Finnish-Americans of Michigan." Even in Britain, Finnegan says, the country-western world was the only one in town that "it seemed appropriate to characterize in class terms at all." The problem is that while the music could be termed "working-class," "that was not how the participants themselves seemed to envisage it" (Finnegan 1989:99). On the one hand, aficionados in Milton Keynes see country-western as "a great leveler," thus not class-specific, while on the other, it is the type of music most involved in the handling of money, hardly an indication of working-class egalitarianism. To return to the Midwest, if polka and country coexist as favorite styles of a putative working class despite their very different origins, association with super-cultural and commodified structures, and relationship to local group heritage, we can only term the music "proletarian" by willful exclusion of a great many contingent factors.

One such factor might be the existence of an internal hierarchy among the groups Keil lumps together as working-class. Though he is comfortable combining white American styles with other ethnic expressive forms to form a large category, insiders like Chicana writer Gloria Anzaldúa (1990:209) see the situation differently: "I grew up feeling ambivalent about our music. Country-western and rock-and-roll had more status." She does confirm Peña's analysis of an *internal* sense of class: "In the 50s and 60s, for the slightly educated and *agringado* Chicanos, there existed a sense of shame at being caught listening to our music." This feeling does not point to a proletarian brotherhood of taste.

Taste itself complicates the location of class in micromusics. According to Leary (1986:3), "'blues tonality' typifies the reed and brass playing of former and present day Wisconsin Bohemian brass bands." Do we simply assume that, because of race, "blues tonality"—at least as widespread in micromusics as the influence of country music or the love of the polka—could not be a part of class orientation in the music of Euro-American subcultures? That assumption would make common sense, but so does the generally accepted feeling that the blues, representing hard times and hard knocks, speaks to the human condition, which might suggest that it suits the "working class." If Wisconsin Bohemian brass-band players are vague on the subject of why they like "blues tonality," on what basis do we assign or not assign class feeling to this particular musical feature? Once again, the question of aesthetics versus social structure makes any hard statement of linkage unlikely.

Within the same constellation of groups and styles, suppose we try out the intersection of religion and class. Take George Dybedal, a Norwegian-American who worked as a "millwright, boilermaker, and welder" and as a lumberjack, certainly presenting a working-class profile. Dybedal sings both Scandinavian and country gospel songs as an amateur, in rest homes and churches, and has put the two together by playing Norwegian hymns accompanied by a guitar style based in "country-western honky-tonk and gospel tunes," with a vocal line that "echoes the church choir" (Leary 1986:20). Leary continues, "The resultant union is illustrative of an important recurrent cultural interplay between ethnic sacred and American secular traditions in the region." I would add that it might well be a class-related set of repertoires, choices, and strategies, but one not much noticed in the literature.

Part of the problem of affirming a class identity for a given style or influence is the constant shifting of micromusical allegiance along the lines of other parameters, such as generation. The Finnish-American musician Leary discusses, Art Moilanen, "rejects contemporary forms regularly heard and played" in his region; "he plays little or no country music from that period following the late 1950s; nor does he play any polka music from much later than the mid-1950s. . . . Art Moilanen's music is, in the 1980s, conservative, a definite throwback, exemplary of cultural lag." For his aging listeners, Moilanen's music "conjures memories of other days—of a 'golden age,' perhaps" (Leary 1987:216). Keil (1982:9, 48) feels that 1950s gritty Chicago polka music represents working-class musicians breaking through the facade of bourgeoisified, recorded polka styles. Perhaps, but this trend would only represent a temporary, local tie-in with class. When the Chicago sound hit the East Coast and changed Northeastern polka style, was it because the locals felt a renewed sense of class orientation when they heard it, or because it was more fun to dance to, or because it appealed to younger polkaphiles? In short, class is contingent on generation, history, and many other factors. Richard Middleton (1990:9) points out that Stuart Hall's "articulating principles" of class position "operate by combining existing elements into new patterns or by attaching new connotations to them." The problem is how to avoid creating a circular argument by looking for the supposed "articulating principles" and then discovering them. Unless we feel that class *must* underlie all cultural expressions, isolating it from all other parameters will be not only difficult but problematic.

Keil gets around this complex of issues simply by asserting that there are proletarian communities, and that as proletarians and as communities, they engage in both the "reworking of older forms" and "the incorporation of contemporary elements." Thus, their "joyful and catholic interest . . . absorbs all that is of use and swiftly eliminates everything not needed" (1984:8). He refines this somewhat tautological approach elsewhere (1982) by noting that ethnicity and class are somehow intertwined. He also interpolates the way individual bandleaders achieve economic success: by blending diverse ethnic traditions. All, however, presumably are still automatically working-class, even though Keil notes in passing that there are serious class differences within the ethnic groups of a single city. In the end, he distills his appeal to class by formulating a "working people's music that's not dependent on state subsidy or corporate mediation" (1982:58), that is, an alternative, though not necessarily oppositional, music. Since working musicians are intimately engaged in commodification, even at a microlevel, only the absence of the big players makes class identification possible. But since the micromusics are infused with products of corporations and are increasingly presented and represented by state-subsidized agencies (e.g., Leary's midwestern publications, the network of folklife festivals), it's still hard to find the direct link between the nature of people's jobs (Keil's definition of class seems to involve "alienation of labor") and the music involved.

Another complication arises from the fact that people—particularly people in a subculture—may try to wish themselves out of their class, and music is a good way to imagine they are somewhere else. Class analysts tend to think of attempts at upward mobility through music as part of hegemony's endless attempt to wipe out traces of opposition through co-opting the subordinate class. The problem is how to paste a class label on the all-American music to which people respond when they turn their backs on their micromusics. Was Lawrence Welk as a superculture standard in a different class (musically and socially) than Lawrence Welk as a North Dakota polka player? Welk earned more than his fans or his midwestern colleagues, but that might not be the place to locate class. On a grid like Bourdieu's, Welk would fit into a class category far from that of patrons of the Metropolitan Opera, but his following is probably as uniform in generation as it is in income and taste. This example raises the issue, elided by Keil, of whether subcultures need to be oppositional, surely a class-related issue in any Marxist tradition. A glance at the patriotic polka song text cited below (p. 92)—which is hardly a unique example—certainly raises doubts. Thanking America "for the freedom and the good life" hardly seems an act of cultural rebellion, any more than using a country-western tune to accompany a Norwegian hymn is necessarily interpolating a working-class counterculture into petit-bourgeois piety.

Suppose we try to isolate a point in time when a community shifts its economic base to gauge the possible effects of class on music. We might consider the period when people gave up house parties for the dancehall atmosphere in which Welk grew up. This change happened somewhere in the 1930s or 1940s in the United States, depending on locale. In northern Vermont, local Saturday night kitchen gatherings gave way to "intercommunity dances at town hall, granges, taverns, and other settings of essentially nondomestic identity" (Carl Bethke in McHale 1981:99). Why this shift occurred is a subject of speculation. Bethke suggests urbanization and the availability of the automobile, possibly class-related factors, as the causes. But the local bandleaders talk about issues of house design—a dance hall was larger than a "small-built living room and a kitchenette"—and of taste. According to a prominent family of musicians, "as country music gained in popularity, the people, especially the young people, lost interest in old time fiddling and dancing and turned to other amusements and social settings" (ibid.:100).

Whether or not the class formation of these Franco-American Vermonters actually shifted during this period and, if so, how important that shift might be for the music are not obvious, nor can we assume that country music should be considered more or less class-related than old-time Franco-American styles. Here again we have the problem of the peculiar nature of country music as being both a superculture product and an appeal to local sentiment at some level of *meaning* rather than point of production or even language of song text, a very attenuated class relationship at best. With the Appadurai perspective, it is possible that ideoscape and ethnoscape are more important than media-, techno- and finanscape in the broad acceptance of country music. Whether or not class is involved remains an open question.

Finally, class analysis is particularly difficult in contemporary societies, where everyone has access one another's musics. Take the Texas-Mexican *conjunto* music that Peña located as class-related within that subculture. By the late 1980s it became available from unrecognized and neighborhood bands in San Antonio, as well as from Los Lobos, originally a local Los Angeles band that has moved into the super-culture stratosphere, (see Lipsitz 1990 for an analysis of this band's strategies) and Linda Ronstadt, an established half German-American, half Mexican-American singer who is usually identified as middle-class. The same music is regularly represented at local, state, and national "folklife" festivals; it was even taken to the Soviet Union in 1990 on that basis. Is it the performer, the arrangements, or some statistically veri-fiable audience that we rate as class-affiliated? Does class reside among the producers, performers, or consumers? Class-ification is a difficult task, given that a broad, mixed-income-level audience of both subcul-tural and mainstream listeners buys the recordings in the United States. Class may be more a matter of reception patterns—how the music is *understood*—than simple analysis of either consumption patterns or even questionnaire-based survey techniques might show if there is a multi-class market. Tastemakers' trends may be more influential than inherited class leanings among listeners, moving us again from the group to the individual. Abroad, the same American music may have other implica-tions, may belong to different social formations.

The somewhat intractable relationship between class and taste crops up throughout the findings of a very pragmatic, purely consumer-oriented methodology developed in the United States to match prod-ucts and target markets. Called the PRIZM system by its inventor, Jonathan Robbin, it divides the country into "clusters," neighborhood types that dot the map, unified by a profile that aligns consumer choices to income level, household type, subcultural ascription, and political leanings, all on the basis of standard sociological measures. As summa-rized in *The Clustering of America* (Weiss 1988), this statistical survey often measures music as a parameter and provides fuel for some diverse positions on the class-taste nexus.

One handy chart shows the top five clusters for music. It reveals that "country" music is listened to mostly by lower-income, rural, predomi-nantly white Americans (although it is also popular in college-based communities, a cluster called "Towns & Gowns"). The table shows that classical music lovers tend to live in upscale areas in and around big cities that have symphonies and classical radio stations. Jazz remains an urban phenomenon largely due to the prevalence of city clubs. As for heavy metal, its listeners supposedly come primarily from upscale family suburbs filled with rebellious teens. Generation, income level, race, and an urban-rural divide play into these profiles and cross-cut them. No one factor predominates. Take the mix of clusters who support jazz at more than twice the national average rate: "Black Enterprise" (white-collar blacks), "Urban Gold Coast" (high-income city whites), "Bohemian Mix" (racially mixed liberals, both high- and low-income, younger and older, taste-driven), "Emergent Minorities" (struggling, working class, predominantly blacks), and "Young Influentials" (white yuppies). Here, race supersedes class as an identifier for blacks, but a mixed-class assortment of whites is just as enthusiastic about jazz. Some of these people are strongly Republican, others are staunch Democrats, the age levels differ sharply. These various clusters have very few, if any, other tastes in common.

One more example from the clustering concept will close this commentary. "New Homesteaders" are moderate- to- low-income white families that have moved from urban to suburban areas and lead an outdoors-oriented life; they prefer country music. "Blue-Collar Nursery" folks have grown up in the same type of suburb and are quite similar to "New Homesteaders" in political outlook and income level, yet they seem attracted to sixties rock. Refining the internal dynamic— one apparently not related to "class" in the normal sense—that leads one cluster to spend its money on country and the other on sixties rock would take significant ethnographic digging of the kind we have yet to see being done for Euro-American local studies.

I have certainly not questioned class as a privileged parameter in micromusics in order to dismiss it, nor the pioneering work of such scholars as Keil and Peña. Class is very relevant if only in terms of the power of the superculture to set the terms, define the scope, of everyone's expressive culture. My intent has been to give some sense of how looking at one variable introduces many others, elbowing any single factor and crowding the frame. Notice, for example, that although I have just quoted women authors and musicians while citing generation, location, and other factors, I have not made a point about "gender." Looking at one variable like class blocks the view, making many concurrent categories invisible. We have not yet found a way to handle more than one major social parameter at a time effectively—or even to do a good job on the one we have chosen to isolate. This real chicken-and-egg paradox I must leave for future theory to rise above.

Let me now return to the search for the subculture, again using Simmel and Finnegan as foils. Neither is very interested in the notion of a bounded unit of the durable, subcultural kind. Simmel somehow jumps from the individual/small affinity-group to the "society." Finnegan points out that a wide variety of small ethnic groups in Milton

Keynes carry on musical activities, but beyond noting the relative isolation of these activities compared with mainstream British forms, she spends no time on them. This backgrounding is revealing of her general enterprise, which is to construct the local basis of a "normal" British musical culture. Her solid citizens do form an impressive bulwark of a highly ramified, articulated, and surprisingly coherent tradition of music-making, especially given that Milton Keynes is a newly developed urban area with only pockets of older communal traditions in preexisting villages. The abundance of local ensembles and events is staggering: this city of about 120,000 souls manages to support 100 choirs, numerous symphony orchestra and chamber groups, 5 to 8 main brass bands, and a dozen folk groups along with 170 rock/pop bands and a vast apparatus of school music-making. Yet this seemingly all-embracing scene represents a local superculture that must make newly arrived Sikh or Vietnamese immigrants feel somewhat alienated, a possibility Finnegan does not entertain or explore; she seems too comfortable with her compatriots to venture across ethnic boundaries, so her detailed presentation does nothing to dissipate the vagueness of the term "subculture," which I have already indicated is not likely to dissipate in these pages.

Still, we might make another attempt at definition by taking a familiar path, the "minority" route, an all-too-comfortable landscape featuring a "majority" population in charge of a state apparatus that defines and tries to control a number of "minorities." A recent volume of comparative essays on minorities (Gold 1984) divides this category into three types: "immigrants" (with "not-so-distant" ancestry elsewhere), "nationals" (long-term residents of nonmajority origin), and "aboriginals" (minorities who were there first), all of whom are covered by the term *ethnicity*, a term of recent origin and much debate. Gold's handy volume offers an important perspective: the view that subcultures are very much defined by the superculture.

This approach works for the state wing of the superculture, which cares very much about any potential competitors "out there" in the society. Whether through mindless bureaucratic efficiency or through coldly calculated patterns of control, governments do a great deal to realize the notion of a subculture; there are important ways in which you can only be a subculture if the authorities say you are, part of a larger location of "identity" in what Stuart Hall (1991) calls "the social imaginary." Yet those ways relate more to the politics and economics of group life and less to its culture. Calling a dozen local groups "Hispanics" in Middletown, Connecticut, certainly puts some pressure on them to respond to that status, but will not necessarily create a unified culture beyond a temporary alliance to obtain the rather meager government funding for cultural activities or to respond to local pressure for minority representation (such as marching in the Memorial Day parade). In the United States, the commercial branch of the superculture is much more effective than is the state in focusing the mediascape and finanscape on supply/demand patterns that dig deeply into cultural consciousness. The resulting ideoscape probably overlaps considerably with the state's view, but not completely, leaving that highly charged, creative space where imagined worlds meet commercial realities. From the industrial point of view, the distinction between immigrant, national, and aboriginal minorities is of little consequence save for the groups' potential as consumers. I devote a whole section below to this sort of superculture-subculture interaction; here the point is to sort out possible ways of understanding just what a subculture might be. The term *minority* is only slightly helpful.

Ethnicity ought to be a beacon as we grope in this darkness. Surely it offers an illuminatory power to define a core of symbolic and expressive experience. Yet ethnicity is turning out to be a light that fails, having quite different meanings across the wide geographic expanse of our survey. Not only are those meanings diverse, but they appear attenuated in two ways: in some places (notably the United States), they are less important than they seem for significant portions of the population, while in others (large parts of Eastern Europe), they gain so much importance that they push toward a sharper sensibility, nationalism. In many middle grounds of Western Europe, it is unclear whether we are talking about *ethnicity* as a general cultural construct, or as just "country of origin" for newcomers or "regional identity" for long-term subcultures. Heisler (1990) notes that while Western Euro-American groupishness of the type we usually label "ethnicity" has proved more resilient than people expected, it is not what we might think. That is, except in isolated, aggravated cases, it represents not a genuine drive for separation or a fierce passion for independent cultural identity, but rather a potential political stance—one among several—from which disenfranchised citizens might choose to negotiate their grievances with the rather tolerant welfare state. Politically viewed, musical expression can easily and naturally form a tactic in such a strategy, or serve merely as a rallying point for latent feelings of identity-flexing. The fact that such musical activities may also attract tourist dollars does not hurt; again, state and commercial interests may converge in terms of defining units of culture. Hugo Zemp (in his *jutz* and *jodel* films of the late 1980s) and Sylvie Bolle-Zemp (1990) have eloquently shown how deeply ideological is the "timeless" Alpine music of Switzerland in its formation and practice, a process also sharply profiled in Ronström's (1989) account of the bag-pipe revival in Sweden. Local and national identities make comfortable bedfellows with sentimental commodification in both contexts. Again, I am trying to emphasize here the need for overlapping perspectives, for multiple viewpoints in sorting out the possible meanings of a given micromusic.

Let us take a closer look at *ethnicity* in the United States, where the term lives in very uneasy cohabitation with the word *race*. From a time before the 1930s, when *race* was the term of choice for all subcultures, to today, when the census makes distinctions among *ethnically* defined populations, nothing has really been clear except the arbitrariness of designations. Mary Waters's recent book *Ethnic Options* (1990) at least provides some guideposts in this terminological wilderness. Having followed up the rich 1980 census data with well-organized interviews among suburban Catholic "whites," Waters arrives at some stimulating suppositions. These people want to be ethnic when common sense sees no reason for it. After all, in recent times there have been few immigrants from their groups (Irish, Slovenian, Italian, and others) and a very high rate of intermarriage. "Assimilation" into a vague Americanism should be the result. Waters conjectures that the reason for this survival of eth-nicity is not a drive for either generational identity or political punch, but the happy chance that this loose form of affiliation allows people to combine the normally dichotomous demands of American society: to belong to a group, a "team," but to be individuals, "different."

Waters implies that for her Euro-Americans, the residual content of ethnicity can often be found in expressive forms: family ceremonies, public occasions, and food. Strangely and somewhat sadly, like many a social scientist, she misses the music in the scene she surveys. Even though she picked the most nonchalant ethnics, none of whom belongs to an ethnic organization, she impoverished her data by leaving out her informants' record collections, if not the music of the weddings they feel so strongly about. What we do learn from Waters is that this type of "white ethnicity" probably does not look like a true "subculture" these days but has some subcultural qualities, of which some kind of *belonging* seems a key component. Perhaps our problem in trying to come up with a comparative perspective hinges on trying to sort out this core verb *belong*, on recognizing its many layers in American society. Waters also points out that this is a variety of belonging. She concludes her study rather caustically by noting that her white Catholic suburbanites stay within the cozy world of their well-established, fellow Euro-American ethnics and therefore have a hard time understanding why things are so complicated for other groups, including "blacks" and "Hispanics." This conclusion strongly implies that for the less comfortable groupings— "blacks" (or perhaps now "African-Americans"), "Hispanics," "Asians," "Native Americans," "Pacific Islanders," to use the superculture's blanket terms—"belonging" has a different resonance.

These "non-Euro-American" social formations are what I call "involuntary" subcultures. They are constrained within well-defined administrative and cultural boundaries established partly through (very different) historical circumstances, but primarily through appearance: you can tell one when you see one, through the superculture's eyes— or, by crude extension, if you've seen one, you've seen them all. At the extreme, this attitude leads to the randomly targeted attacks that dot the American social landscape: "Let's kill a ——— today" is an idea that actually occurs to certain citizens. This notion of subculture is as flexible as any other, in the sense that it does not depend only on skin color. Typical dress/hairstyle (Orthodox Jews), hangouts, or body behavior (homosexuals) can guide the attacker to the victim: what are taken to be essential features will suffice, features which thus stand out in stark relief as not just inherited traits or adopted manners, but as major signal systems in the semiotics of society. Identification comes from all sides: individuals, government, and industry, with the latter more interested in a target market than a target for assault (though the recent furor over a type of cigarette aimed at African-Americans implied that the two may be interchangeable). At one level, then, we are dealing with *recognizable* groups, if only in the literal sense of the word. However, any relief at achieving a definition should be short, for we are interested in only one aspect of these people's lives, their music. The articulation between the externally defined packaging and the actual lived experience of those in "the group" may be—and frequently is—mapped for a series of linkages, but it remains equally elusive for others. For every explicit association of a community's music with its essence, there is a supercultural move to generalize the style and erase, if not deny, the connection. Conversely, for every confident statement about how "black music" is tied to "black culture," there are eloquent silences that acknowledge the autonomy of aesthetic choices, for individuals, small group, and even sizable "minorities" (which may have twenty-five million members).

The situation is just as complex in terms of gender, which I left suspended a while back. The attempt of ethnomusicology to grapple with this major factor in world music-making has done little more than lay out a number of local situations in which gender plays a role in certain contexts. Euro-America remains less described, especially outside "traditional" peasant/postpeasant contexts, than other world regions. Despite two anthologies (Koskoff 1987, Herndon and Ziegler 1990), music remains unintegrated with either the achievements of earlier feminist theory or the more recent multidisciplinary move into gender studies. Even in the most recent survey (Koskoff 1991), the stress is on issues of "power" within a dichotomous male-female social order rather than on the cultural construction of a more nuanced category that intersects with many other variables (race, class, religion, and so forth), admittedly a theoretical task the scanty available data can hardly help to solve.

My own sole foray into gender studies (Slobin 1990a) part of a large historical-ethnographic study of the American cantorate, brought this gap home to me. Women first officially entered the profession in 1976 within the Reform denomination of American Judaism, in 1989 in the Conservative denomination, so the issue could be tightly framed. The fact that a woman could stand before a congregation as an aesthetic-spiritual ritual leader seemed a profound shift in an ancient religion. Yet as subcultural practice, this new en-gendering of an old music profession turned out to be closely linked to supercultural norms. That the action took place at all was a result of the concurrent drive within Protestant American religious life to empower women in leadership roles. And within the Jewish world, gender turned out to be no more prominent than professionalism itself among the female cantors interviewed. The cantorate is strongly split between ubiquitous part-timers, who lead services once a week or only once a year at the time of the High Holidays, and full-time, salaried professionals, who have with great difficulty wrung middle-class working conditions and respectability from synagogues only since the 1950s. These hard-won gains create an often bitter gulf between the part-time and full-time women, often overriding the question of feminism or gender roles among the practitioners. Among congregants, supercultural social trends seem to be speeding the acceptance of women as cantors, so the issue is much more muted than might be anticipated when, for example, a 150-year old synagogue hires its first woman for the job. While it is perhaps not surprising that gender is no more separable than any other factor in a complex of micromusical practice, I do not think we have enough of a feel as yet for how gender does function within subcultural settings to understand its importance. For most Euro-American micromusics, gender becomes most obvious by its absence, since the literature seems drawn magnetically to many spheres of male activism without defining them as male and still scants women's distinctive contribution in contexts where it counts.

One final note on levels of analysis. The more I look at subcultural scenes, the more impressed I am with *internal* supercultures that create a layer of definition and control that is exquisitely articulated with the mainstream system of management, both state and industrial. Hispanic cable television and major radio stations consistently ignore the many subgroups within the vast multiethnic listenership covered by their sanctioned ethnic umbrella. Even in the smallest, white American micromusical worlds, ambitious community leaders dictate musical trends and allocate scarce resources arbitrarily. A major plane of analysis lies solely within localized settings, where even "micromusic" seems an overblown and contestable term. Thus any attempt to define a musical subculture for even the most clearly identified groups will fall into the cracks we've been exploring: between the individual, the local formation, and the wider setting.

Having run through some of the problems of levels of analysis, I have no blueprint for the micromusical home. For the present, all I mean to do beyond critique is to suggest that we work on defining three overlapping spheres of cultural activity: "choice," "affinity," and "belonging."

Choice. Simmel suggests that individual choice is crucial for isolated individuals. This view is in direct opposition to the model of cultural pluralism (cf. Niles 1978 on being Latvian), in which everyone starts off life in a recognizable subculture that spreads out from a nuclear family and is based in heritage and locale. If we combine these two perspectives, we can say that we all grow up with *something*, but we can choose just about *anything* by way of expressive culture. Part of the reason for this eclecticism is that we start with many "somethings." My father's song repertoire, for example, draws on a huge range of childhood sources, from Russian and Yiddish folk and popular songs through Jewish liturgy and Christian chestnuts learned at a YMCA camp to American vaudeville and popular songs. Leary's copper-range Scandinavians and Texas Czechs are similarly eclectic, and the teenagers of Milton Keynes are as likely to find affinities with imported sounds as with older British pop. Today, the range of musical experience grows ever wider in Euro-American societies, so the gap between a supposed musical lineage and free choice constantly narrows. For the West, this supports newer trends like world beat; for the former East, breadth means being able to go beyond bootlegged diversity to the world of open-market consumerism. Choices have to be made; everyone is exposed to too much to take it all at face value. After all, the root meaning for *eclectic* has to do with selection, choosiness.

Affinity. We come now to affinity, so essential to understanding choice, so necessary for affiliation, for choices are not random. At least, so the observer hopes, for we prefer pattern. Yet in the conditions of modern diversity, we may have to assume, rather than prove, affinity, since evidence may be hard to come by. Take the case of a student of mine who, after simply hearing a Highland bagpipe band outside her window, became so attracted to the music that she became a professional piper, not an easy task for a woman in the 1970s. This "pathway" is a type that Finnegan does not explore. Do we psychologize this evident affinity, or do we invoke a kind of cultural Brownian motion, a random activity of musical free electrons attaching themselves to any available nucleus?

All that is clear at this point is that strong attractions exist, and they fall into the type of affiliation-web Simmel describes. The overlap of memberships can be striking, going against any simple formulation of heritage equals membership, or even membership A implies membership B. Contradance enthusiasts in southern New England may also belong to groups that perform "vintage" dances (nineteenth- and early twentieth-century popular styles), as well as groups that do square dance, Scottish country dance, or even reconstructions of the eighteenth-century English social dances of John Playford. The listing confounds any sense of belonging out of regional revivalism or ethnic orientation. The only affinity seems to be to dance itself, and at one dance, 80 percent of respondents reported belonging to two or more groups (Hast, conversation, 1990).

Belonging. A choice to follow up an affinity leads to belonging. Yet belonging is itself a complex act. How deep does it go—casual participant, part-time organizer, professional musician? Patterns of commitment can be intensive or desultory for leisure-time affinity groups and even within ethnic collectives. For groups with flexible, playful boundaries, it's easy to be very Latvian one month, and unmarked American the next. Even for members of what I have called "involuntary" groups, whose physical appearance puts them permanently in a state of boundary awareness, the kinds and degrees of affiliation seem numberless. Belonging is not only situational in the face of challenges, but personal. Expressive culture is both what "we" do and what "I" do—and, as Simmel points out, the two are so intertwined as to be inextricable. To sneak the superculture back into the discussion, it is also what "they" do. No cultural rule says that people cannot pay allegiance to small, medium, and large groups simultaneously, and, as Simmel says, this option may be very attractive to individuals, who can locate themselves variably—

hence comfortably—in different groups. A blues scholar once told me that when he interviewed a venerable singer, the old musician cited Al Jolson as one of his models. This statement may be politically incorrect but musically plausible.

There are times when we should invoke the power of hegemony, but other times when the superculture seems to be just another strand in the web of group affiliations, chosen out of aesthetic affinity. Indeed the superculture itself is not a free-standing structure; as Finnegan (1989:184) notes, "the national framework affected local groups and players, but . . . there was also a sense in which the large national and commercial interests were themselves dependent upon the grass-roots musical tradition." Al Jolson, of course, starred in a supercultural scene that took old blues singers into account as source material.

To find some critical distance from the Western Euro-American world that Simmel and Finnegan represent, it might be useful to look at the social organization of subcultural music-making in the former USSR, using the suggestive model that Eduard Alekseev (1988:169) developed just as the whole system was about to collapse. He identifies four types of micromusical life: musical folklore, professional music of the oral tradition, musical *samodeiatel'nost'*, and composers' music. Musical folklore roughly overlaps with our commonsense category of folk music. Professional music of the oral tradition is something like what ethnomusicologists used to (and still tend to) call a "classical" or "art" music outside the Western tradition, although it might also include certain kinds of professional folk musicians who stand out from the crowd of average music-makers in a peasant or nomad society. *Samodeiatel'nost'* is hard to describe, being a creature of the Soviet superculture. Translated roughly as "do-it-yourselfness," the term covered (and probably still will, for some time to come) a wide range of local, state-encouraged musical activities by amateur collectives. Composers' music is the work of officially recognized, schooled, "classical" or "serious" composers. The table summarizes the distinctions among the four varieties in Alekseev's formulation.

Alekseev's scheme is quite society-specific, relying on the reader's tacit knowledge of a complex supercultural system—now being reorganized into national music cultures—of music organization, including all-Union, republic, and local administrators, institutions, and systems of support/reward. Traces of an old Marx/Engels/Leninist understanding of levels of culture and their evolution under socialism shine through the rubrics: terms like *professional* and *oral tradition* are not innocent, but are rather freighted with notions of class conflict and "inevitable"

	Musical folklore	Professional oral tradition	*Samodeiatel'nost'* groups	Composers' music
Creative method	nonspecialized	specialized	nonspecialized, nonprofessional	specialized, professional
Origins	contextual, situated	autonomous	autonomous	autonomous
Circulation	esoteric	esoteric, exoteric	open	open
Means of preservation	oral	oral	written	written
Manner of production	varied, multiple	varied, multiple	mainly opuslike	opus
Form of artistic consciousness	collective	collective, individual	largely collective	individual
Relationship to audience	unmediated	unmediated	mediated, unmediated	mediated

stages of social evolution that space does not allow me to unpack here. The outsider's lesson I'd like to draw from the table does not require a long excursus on Soviet musical life. Simply put, I'd like to point to the interrelationship of suggested factors from the perspective of searching for the subculture in an elaborate, bureaucratized scheme that refuses to admit such a term, preferring instead the vague *narodnaia*, which can mean both "folk" and "national" (but not "subcultural"), as the adjective for *muzyka*, itself the very inchoate word *music* that does not specify degree of distribution, variety of genre, or amount of local attachment.

Alekseev's chart does at least hint at differences between individual and collective inventions and performances, esoteric and exoteric knowledge, and mediated and unmediated transmission patterns; it also tells us that items can be packaged ("opuslike") or flexible ("variable"). All of these clues suggest the existence of multiple levels of local, group-specific attitudes and approaches. His job in describing how an entire music culture operates is, in a way, easier than mine, since he could begin with more clearly articulated bureaucratic/ideological structures. For example, to each category of individual and group, the state dispensed a hierarchy of awards and medals, as well as a broad range of other perks, like facilities and touring possibilities. The whole structure is, in a sense, simpler to analyze administratively than musically.

Take a notion like *samodeiatel'nost'*, which is *largely* individual, mediated *or* unmediated, *mainly* opuslike in its repertoire. It may be nonprofessional and nonspecialized, but that description is a simplification, both categories having a rather technical sense in a largely noncommodified music system. Here a single bureaucratic term can act like a handy broom that sweeps untidy heaps of uncomfortable diversity under the large rug of the cultural commissar's office. It is very much a home-grown term. For the rest of Euro-America, *samodeiatel'nost'*, though it looks like merely "home-made music," would cover too many types of music-making to be a useful empirical category; the word really needs a whole monograph, and it would repay the effort.

In the American context, we might begin by defining it as those organizations worthy of funding and recognition from the National Endowment for the Arts, the Smithsonian Institution, or the Library of Congress, but such a delimitation would be altogether too exclusive: many commercially oriented groups have a "do-it-yourself" quality that *samodeiatel'nost'* implies. Yet if we boil down this system to its essentials, the situation is not all that different from the Western Euro-American scene described earlier. We are dealing with an interplay of individual, ensemble, subculture, and superculture. An implicit hierarchy of musics, which is partly articulated through state support networks and which puts "classical" music at the top, held for both the Soviet and Western worlds.

Of course, unlike the Western superculture, the Soviet superculture had no competition from industry, and subcultures were much more rigidly determined; individual choice, because of the poverty of the techno- and mediascapes, remained more limited in the USSR. Yet control by the state in the late socialist years seemed to have become less effective than in earlier times, local culture often being a harbinger of change. A closer look at the mechanism that supported *samodeialtel'nost'* shows extensive cracks in the structure of hegemony that perhaps presaged its collapse. The "House of Culture," a Stalinist mechanism for showcasing and controlling local culture, was exported to all Eastern bloc countries but it tended to be weakest when it came to music. White (1990:72) proposes that "the transitory nature of an arts performance as compared for example with a book, makes it much harder to enforce censorship regulations." Economically, too, local houses of culture needed to augment stingy state subsidies by selling tickets to concerts that people really wanted to attend. But in general, the 1980s saw a decline in the basic significance of this regulative recreational outlet, with amateur art activity moving to the home from the House of Culture, partly because of what even an official commentator had to call "an allergy towards official forms of cultural-leisure events and their content" (ibid.:148). Understanding this complex interplay of local taste, nationally imposed trends, public and private activities, and many other factors would require more ethnographic study of the old East than any-one has done. In terms of the present rubric, "belonging," just what do former Soviet/East European music-makers "belong" to at present? The war between allegiances—state, local, "national," "ethnic"—is just beginning to come to a boil, with uncertain consequences for music.

The foregoing attempt at tinkering with levels of analysis and trying to sort out the relative independence of variables is just a sketch. A more comprehensive methodology must be deferred until we have a better grasp of choice, affinity, belonging, and the intense interplay of all three, for a number of societies, in terms of several parameters: (1) the sphere of the individual, a one-person group with an intense inner aesthetic life that draws on any and all available sources; (2) the charmed circle of the affinity group, a jointly imagined world that arises from a set of separate strivings temporarily fused at a moment of common musical purpose; (3) the overlapping, intersecting planes of multiple group activities that may range across a wide scale of magnitude, ideology, and audience. To pretend to a clarity of analysis of any musical grouping, moment, style, or context is to bypass this complexity for the sake of oversimplification or even outright essentialism. And, as I argue next, staying within the bounds of any particular society provides a very limited point of view: enter the interculture.

CHAPTER FOUR

Interpolating the Interculture

❖

There is a plane of analysis that extends beyond the issues of the lively, charged, and even tumultuous interaction of parts of a "society" within nation-state bounds. This is the perspective of the far-flung, expansive reach of musical forces that cross frontiers. For this vantage point I've adopted the compatible term *interculture*, no easier to define and describe than the earlier words. In fact, though I started by thinking I was coining a term, I've seen it appear rather comfortably in a variety of writings, used variously, of course. My strategy once again is to talk around the term until a profile, or at least a problem, emerges.

At present, I visualize three types of intercultures. The first, the *industrial interculture*, is the creature of the commodified music system that popular music commentators often cast as a monster, a corporate octopus whose tentacles stretch menacingly across the world, dominating local scenes and choking off competition. In a more measured way, Wallis and Malm's (1984) classic study of the international phonogram industry paints the picture of a somewhat confused cartel that unhesitatingly uses its hegemonistic powers to intervene in local musical worlds. The researchers deliberately chose small countries as their database, a choice that maximizes the importance of the big boys on the block. The issue of the survival of local creativity is foregrounded, and the interculture becomes a kind of large-scale superculture, where whole societies act the role of subcultures. Of particular interest is the fact that for small countries at this level of analysis, musical scenes differ little: "Even a study of developments from around 1900 to the early 1970s in countries as different as Sweden, Tanzania, Tunisia, and Trinidad shows interesting similarities in the patterns of change within their music cultures," note Wallis and Malm (ibid.:12), though the changes are staggered across the decades, with Sweden feeling them the earliest.

In trying to account for this similarity among disparate nations, Wallis and Malm (ibid.:17) cite a triad of ideoscape ("value systems and knowledge spread through the European education system"), technoscape ("changes in the economic and production systems"), and, most recently, mediascape—the new mass media, magnified in their impact because of the small populations involved. This schema fits right in with two current intellectual trends. The first is to see the "master narrative" of the Enlightenment as crucial to the spread of a global culture based on portable principles of education and liberal democracy, a view not invented by, but well popularized by Anderson (1983). The second tendency is to stress the role of the technoscape as the handmaiden of monopoly capitalism. Yet Wallis and Malm also detail the enormous role of a handful of local enthusiasts, who act as counterweights to the mass of the media. They end on an ambiguous note as to who will prevail: the giants or the pygmies. The ethnoscape seems to be of great importance, and there may be more than one ideoscape in sight in these countries.

In fact, the industrial interculture plays with two partners: the consumer and the state; when all three players sit down to the table, power plays, bluffs, strategies, and reactions create a very complex game. For the consumer's perspective, we would need more reception studies than we have, and we have very few indeed. Even the little that we know indicates that despite the homogeneity of the product, the diversity of its reception is striking. The local domestication of Anglo-American rock music by European regions, from Slovenia (Barber-Kersovan 1989) and Italy (Fabbri 1989) and the German-speaking lands (Larkey 1989) to the former Eastern bloc (Ryback 1990; Troitsky 1987) is an eye-opening, if uneven and disorganized, field of research. A quick survey shows how localized the impact of the presumed rock juggernaut has been, as it changes course to fit the local musical roadways and the traffic conditions of each society, including such widely varied factors as the presence of well-entrenched regional styles that refuse to give way; the typecasting of rock as the property of a certain subculture, political group, or generation; and the benign or hostile effects of governmental interference, intervention, and control. As Larkey (1989) puts it, "previous assumptions of increasing ethnic and cultural homogeneity . . . need to be re-examined as new cultural traditions, language usages . . . and musical innovations have emerged in response to the challenge posed by the internationalization of culture."

Some phases of this process, such as an early period of listening only to Anglo-American bands, followed by an attempt to create a local counterpart, repeat themselves in more than one society. This sequence happened in the 1970s in German-speaking countries, much later in the Soviet Union, where only in the late 1980s did graffiti praising Soviet rock groups began to compete for attention with the ubiquitous wall writings in honor of Western groups like the Beatles (Bushnell 1990:97).

The state is not a passive player in this expansion of intercultures. Larkey (1989), for example, points out a complex intermeshing of governmental and industrial guidance in West and East Germany, Austria, and Switzerland. Even in a liberal Western democracy like Sweden, a government commitee made the following statement in 1976: "it is important that the state is continually aware of technical advances and is able to take action to direct the results of those developments into channels consistent with the aims of state cultural policy" (quoted in Wallis and Malm 1984:11).

The industrial interculture is no easier to pin down than any other hegemonic force, subject to internal fracturing and widely differing buffeting forces, forced to make compromises, co-opt competition, and come up with new strategies to make a living. For example, it was by no means clear that a category of "ethnopop/world beat/world music" should or could emerge in the late 1980s, with the potential to recast whole studio and production practices in the intercultural economy and ideology. Although empirical evidence is lacking, the movement seems to have come from the grass roots, rather than from the top down, though the industry was, as usual, adroit in co-opting the trend; according to Krister Malm (personal communication, 1990), in 1986 a group of recording company executives decided that "world music" was a definable and viable style category. Frith (1988) has pointed out that the concept of a global style pool has in fact reshaped the way the industry works. Instead of building up groups through the studio system, producers (who might be outsiders like Paul Simon or David Byrne) can simply identify, shape, and promote available talent worldwide. This may just be the old industrial octopus with a new suit on, but the ramifications for world musical sensitivities and the role of local music-makers might be profoundly changed. Aggressive self-fashioning and promotion, as in the Guadeloupe group Kassav's invention of commercial *zouk* music cited earlier, now fits into a global marketing scheme rather than playing itself out as insignificant local energy co-opted, then abandoned, by the major labels.

Another limitation on the monolith model is the internal activity of groups whose music is commodified. For South Asians in Britain, Banerji (Banerji and Baumann 1990:141) found that "the South Asian music market proceeded to evolve in its own way, largely independent of the mainstream music economy, reflecting, perhaps, the isolation of the community at large, and increasing that of its musicians." This study includes surprising statistics: "piracy may have accounted in 1988 for some 25 per cent only of cassettes played at home" (ibid.:149), threatening the existence of "legitimate" companies. A case like that of *bhangra*, the genre Banerji and Baumann describe, is very instructive in revealing the complexities that the industry faces when intruding in subcultural music production. Their account stresses the aggressiveness of internal self-definition and promotion techniques in the face of the interest shown by the "majors'" in finding a crossover value to a style that might then be marketed to the mainstream.

Mentioning this type of in-group activity brings us to the second type of interculture: the *diasporic interculture*, which emerges from the linkages that subcultures set up across national boundaries. One way of visualizing this variety of interculture is to imagine North America and Europe as a set of clear plastic overlays on a political map. We would use a different color for the distinctive network of each subculture, connecting the dots of population concentration: Yugoslavs, Greeks, Jews, Indians, Chinese, Gypsies, and so on. The thick, colorful pileup of overlays would eventually describe the grand diasporic interculture pattern of our region, with lines stretching off the map to the other continents. We have only a sketchy sense of how these scattered populations keep in touch with and influence each other, though case studies are starting to accumulate.

One point should be stressed: there is no simple relationship to a "homeland." Gold's 1984 survey of diasporic situations provides a nice foil for this issue; there, the term *mother country* is favored. Right off, the editor points out that while the mother country is quite important to people, "not much attention has been paid to its meanings" (1). He also immediately identifies the notion of mother country as being controlled by insiders, not outsiders, "not just a label attached to an immigrant— its imagery is very much his (her) property" (2). We have no systematic way to explore how that imagery—what Anderson might call an "imagined community"—is created or evolves over time. But there are even greater challenges to working on diasporic scenes: there might be not just one mother country. As Paul Gilroy (1987) has argued cogently, for blacks in Great Britain, we must take into account African, Caribbean, and African-American influences, and the four-sided perspective holds when looking at the other three regions of this multiple diaspora.

Such diasporic networks are very distinctive and have a complex internal structure. While they may make a point-to-point connection with a homeland population and style, they might also conjure up new networks abroad. Let us take the case of *bhangra* in Britain just cited. According to Banerji (1990:139), "it is performed and enjoyed by Punjabis of Sikh, Hindu, Muslim, Jain and Christian religious orientations throughout the India-Pakistan borderlands." Since the Punjabis "dominate the cultural scene among South Asians in Britain, a community that includes, among others, Sylhettis from Bangla Desh, Gujaratis, Bengalis, Tamils, and the descendants of South Asians who had previously emigrated to east Africa," Banerji states, the boundaries of *bhangra* have spread to many representatives of South India abroad. Its popularity also means that its network extends to "the USA, east Africa and Australasia" (137). Part of the success of this mushrooming genre of the mid-1980s lies in the eclecticism of Punjabi culture itself, "rooted in a region characterized by immense cultural diversity and intense cross-fertilization for most of its history" (138). We can view these Punjabis from the same perspective I found helpful in trying to understand the ability of Jewish musicians to move from immigrant tenements to recording studios and Hollywood almost instantaneously, using their homegrown versatility to good effect. Eclecticism is a handy cultural resource.

Another vantage point for diasporic networking is that of the individual. Consider the case of Fikret, a Turkish musician living in Sweden, as described to me by Anders Hammerlund (personal communication, 1990). Fikret is trying to create an individual fusion of Turkish and Western musics, which creates a "very complicated and ambiguous situation," since the Swedes see him as a representative of Turkish folk music, which they are glad to support as a good liberal superculture does for its minorities. However, Fikret has learned his Turkish music mostly in Sweden since he comes from a family for whom music would have been an unacceptable choice of profession. Meanwhile, the Turks in Sweden have not much use for his music but have backed his state-supported record as a matter of ethnic pride. Finally, Fikret's work is returning to his homeland, where it has helped "pave the way for music as an independent field of social activity." Cases like Fikret's show just how complex the relationship of even a single musician to his place of origin can be, when the putative "homeland" has to be understood as a complex of locales, styles, and even families. At the same time, the "host country"—or is it his new "homeland"?—has offered him a new imagined community (Anderson 1983) or even a structure of feeling (Williams 1977) by opening up a creative space denied by the "homeland." Meanwhile, his relationship to his compatriots in emigration is problematic, since their "homeland" ideals as well as their notions of proper Turkishness while abroad seem to differ sharply from his.

That nothing is simple in the world of diasporic music-making is elegantly illustrated by the anthology called *Klangbilder der Welt*, produced by the International Center for Comparative Musicology and Documentation in (former West) Berlin. More than 150 musical organizations in the city were contacted and interviewed extensively. Nearly all the groups represent diasporic intercultural networks, but the range of approaches and histories of formation, activity, and stylistic choice is enormous, a data bank too rich to summarize easily here. One of the parameters of present interest might be the extent to which the groups stay within community bounds or try to reach out to a wider population of both other diasporic groups and Germans. A complementary factor is whether ensemble membership is all-immigrant or part German. As in Swedish situations, this mixture within diasporic music-making can be a result of the infectious nature of the sounds/cultures or can simply be the outcome of a shortfall of newcomer musicians, requiring Europeans (or Americans in U.S. examples) to fill out ensembles to the proper size.

As in all diasporic contexts, musical scenes vary according to how those abroad think of those "back home." In the United States, we have the long history of the older immigrant groups, like the Germans and Irish, to document the way musics are tied to politics. Both cases are complicated. For the Germans, the fact that the United States twice went to war with the homeland led to many a twist and turn in ethnic music-making; here the superculture set the tone of internal evolution. Yet back in the "simpler" days of the nineteenth century, the German community was more concerned with their own crises, like the war with the Danes, which passed without much comment in mainstream America (though it was likely noted among Danish-Americans). For the Irish, the tortured relationship to English hegemony has remained a major point of orientation for 150 years, spawning countless songs and marking the careers of innumerable musicians. For more recent groups, the situation is similar. Lithuanian- (and other Baltic-) Americans have for over half a century identified with the cause of the "captive nations," seeing themselves as victims of a colonizing Russia. This perspective brought them into an alliance with like-minded Ukrainians, who may appear at the same concert events. The slow emergence of a new national identity for the Baltic states has caused a seismic ripple through the Lithuanian community, making itself felt in expressive culture. "Were there to be an independent homeland, how would we relate to it?" is a new question, so that a homegrown event or a concert by a visiting Lithuanian rock group has a resonance in 1991 that was not there in 1981. Meanwhile, Americans who have grown up as Lithuanian Scouts find, on visiting Vilnius, that they can teach ethnic traditions to the friends they make there, since the scouts have been banned in Lithuania for fifty years (Julija Gelaziš, personal communication, 1991).

It is particularly striking that, unlike the industrial interculture, many diasporic musical scenes, involve this sort of oral transmission—real, old-fashioned, face-to-face contact—as well as disembodied modes of communication. When Arab-Americans in Detroit or Yugoslavs in Germany absorb their music live, it has a subtly different meaning as cultural nourishment, akin to preparing dishes from fresh ingredients instead of eating out of a can. Measuring yourself as an immigrant or "ethnic" against a group of homeland musicians who are standing right in front of you is not the same as flipping on a cassette of disembodied voices from somewhere in space and time, just as in America, talking to an anonymous telephone operator at an undisclosed location reached by an 800 number is not the same as interacting with a live salesperson in a store.

Take the example of Mike Orlich of Wakefield, Wisconsin, on the shores of Lake Superior, hardly a center of Serbian culture. His experience and impact are recounted by Jim Leary:

Mike first heard tamburitza music in south Chicago in 1937 after hitchhiking from Upper Michigan. In 1946 Pete Markovich of Milwaukee toured the Gogebic Range and showed Mike how to play and where to order tamburitza instruments. Orlich keeps up on the latest developments in the tamburitza field, buying mail order records and tapes and attending the Tamburitza Extravaganza, an annual convention of tamburitza combo musicians. Thus he has taught the orchestra many newer popular numbers from Yugoslavia, a comparative repertory among Slavic musicians of the north country. (Leary 1986:17)

Here the commodified, mail order side of networking plays a less important role than the direct contact among like-minded musicians. Hitchhiking hundreds of miles just to make a linkage is a strong expression of commitment, fortified by the annual pilgrimage to a micromusical convention.

Live transmission does not have to be confined to in-group situations. Latin American refugees teaching protest songs to reindeer herders in Norway also engage in intense diffusion of musics through an intercultural network. One of the world's most widely spread songs is "We Shall Overcome"; I doubt that many of the millions from South Africa to Japan who have sung it learned it from a sound recording. In fact, the spread of the protest song, from its roots in American union/ left-wing/civil rights soil through its flowering in Latin American *nueva cancion*, implies a third type of interculture, a global political, highly musical network that has not been comprehensively studied. It is somewhat allied with the postpeasant "folk" music movement, which drew inspiration from the American "folk revival" and grew to dominate a certain segment of youth music across Europe.

Bands from many lands learn from each other's records, but more profoundly from direct contact at the many festivals that sprang up to service a transnational performer-audience interest group. Such situations seem to ask for a third type of cross-cutting system, which I tentatively title the *affinity interculture*. Musics seem to call out to audiences across nation-state lines even when they are not part of a heritage or a commodified, disembodied network, and particularly when the transmission is of the old-fashioned variety—face to face, mouth to ear. Just as within modern societies Simmel could find that affinity groups are powerful and tenacious for the average citizen, so contemporary global culture allows anyone anywhere to be attracted to musics of choice, many of which can now be heard close to home.

The mobility of youth in the Euro-American world since the 1960s has accelerated this rather random bonding of individuals to musics. Any "folk" festival has a lively interactive scene of tradition-transfer just outside the concert hall or even built in as "workshops." The ever-larger Falun Folk Festival in Sweden now has a week-long camp for children where young Scandinavians absorb as much as possible about style and outlook from several visiting musicians'. The year I saw it, it was simply called "Ethno 90," turning one of our favorite cultural prefixes into a festival event. The rhetoric of the advance flyer for the 1991 youth music camp spells out four goals for the fifteen- to twenty-five-year-olds being solicited by the Falun Folk Festival and the Swedish branch of Jeunesse Musicales:

—create contacts and understanding between young people from different countries and cultures through music;
—give vitality to a music culture generally not associated with youth culture;
—stimulate a world ethnic music culture full of nuances;
—strengthen heritage and cultural identity among young people.

This statement could of course be seen as a supercultural move; certainly the rhetoric is resonant with the phrases of liberal democracies, cultural pluralism, and intercultural goodwill that we associate with administrative pronouncements. Yet the Falun Folk Festival does not emanate from the state, and although the Jeunesse Musicales' international network is given as a resource, it is not an intercultural bureaucracy on the order of the major phonogram companies. Most important, the camp promises direct exposure to and exchange of musics in a deliberately countercultural manner; no profit motive or hegemony move is apparent on the surface, and the creation of an affinity group seems the immediate goal despite the heady verbiage about eventual benefits.

Hearing one another's music or even playing in one another's bands, as in Berlin, Stockholm, or Massachusetts, has led to new ways of music-making among groups that play at the same concerts or festivals, whether in the city itself or while on tour abroad. Even a nation as huge as the United States has a number of well-developed venues and circuits at which representatives of diasporic micromusics meet. Often enough, the superculture lends a hand by creating such contexts, like the annual American Folklife Festival in Washington, D.C. Of course, record stores also provide food for musical thought; both industrial and diasporic intercultures are available in both live and disembodied versions in any given locale. A city, festival, or shop can create a musical world without frontiers, one that seems to exist across, or somehow suspended above, national lines, to stretch my definition of interculture even further.

A tendency to very particular intercultural affinities may even be a national tradition. Kealiinohomoku (1986:119) states that "the most ardent of non-American would-be Indians are Germans," who support "hundreds of Western lore clubs." Germany has had a well-grounded institutional framework since the end of the nineteenth century, when Germans were influenced by Karl May's novels about a fictitious Native American hero. Such affinity groups can even create new intercultural patterns: "Some Indian servicemen who were stationed in Germany have been inspired to research Indian cultures after finding themselves the subject of adulation."

Ultimately, like the other -cultures, the interculture needs to be looked at from an individual perspective: it is not only around us and between us, but inside us. This play of meaning at many levels of societies and among its various strata of cultural production leads me to move from a consideration of my -culture terms to a closer look at how they interact as a final overview for this section.

The only way the -cultures exist at all is through interaction. That is a statement of faith or, at the least, of current thinking, which tends to deny essentialism, avoid reductionism, affirm the situational. I have no quarrel with that stance. It means that we should take a bird's-eye view of interaction before coming down to earth for close-up analysis of subcultural practice.

Of course, there are several slants on interaction. If we see things in terms of struggle and strategy, we identify the political dimension of expressive culture and foreground the conflict between superculture and both subculture and interculture. This is not hard to do. Evidence abounds of attempts by both the state and industry to manage people's music-making. There are many tools at the disposal of controlling or repressive forces. Governments can use carrot-and-stick approaches through funding, setting regulatory agencies to work to monitor and master the airwaves, enacting restrictive legislation, enforcing statutes through the judicial system—and, in the United States, does this through three overlapping and competing levels of government (local, state, and federal). I write this statement at the outset of the 1990s, when the American habit of cyclical application of such control has moved into a well-publicized and coordinated movement for state intervention in "the arts," from the Congress to the local sheriff, with a strong ripple effect out to the private wings of the superculture (foundations, publishers, the entertainment industry).

When the state intervenes, it denies any intention to interfere with the expression of subcultures, appealing to general principles of decency, unity, history. Yet subcultures strike back, sensitive to encroachment, creating interaction, trying to disarm through dialectic rather than remain silent. The 1990 case of the rap group 2 Live Crew, judged obscene by local authorities, is a classic case in point. African-American commentators attempted to cast the case in a discourse of subcultural meanings and rights: the sexual hyperbole that was seen as a threat by judges and the police became a logical extension of black street talk, and the band itself challenged white authorities to clamp down on equally bad-talking white acts. Spokespeople for African-American expressive culture rejected as selective and ethnocentric the seemingly neutral notion of universal standards of decency and the Supreme Court's policy of allowing local criteria of obscenity to prevail, creating a superculture-subculture confrontation. The fury on both sides shows just how seriously everyone takes "entertainment."

Classic control situations are an extreme form of interaction. At the opposite end of the spectrum lies the superculture's ability to effect an *erasure* of interchange. This erasure occurs in subtle ways, as in the strict guidelines for plots that children's book publishers demand of writers, or the self-imposed rating system of the film industry, or, now, record producers. Often subcultural voices are unheard because of the seemingly natural laws of the marketplace: ethnic broadcasting is transient and weak simply because of the way advertising dollars flow, down sidestreams into the main channels rather than the reverse.

Between control and erasure lies a vast domain of interaction among all units of the society and out into the intercultures. Interplay can take many surprising turns, as in the case of how micromusics should deal with enthusiasts such as the people Kealiinohomoku (1986:111) calls "would-be Indians" in the United States, who for generations have engaged in institutionalized imitation of Native American life through agencies like the Boy Scouts. She notes, "Some Indians endorsed this romanticized appreciation of their cultures, while others resented it. Still others were uncomfortable with the resulting paradoxes." As one Native American puts it, "Can you imagine a group of non-Christian children pretending they are Catholic for an evening once every two weeks . . . taking communion, making a crucifix, or saying Hail Mary?" (115).

Although less relevant for indigenous peoples overwhelmed by newcomers, in most cases, supercultures and subcultures are, historically and structurally, built from each other. Chapman, McDonald, and Tonkin (1989:18) argue that, "it is clear that 'ethnic groups' and 'nations' are of the same stock." However, studying interaction means looking at both sides, and ethnographers of all persuasions have their biases: "We might feel . . . that the study of nations was implied and required by the study of ethnic groups. It remains true, however, that anthropologists have tended to be happy to study ethnic groups, and have been much less happy studying nations, as if the latter were defined out of their vision and capacities" (ibid). Surveying the totality of the ideology and lived musical experience from both the supercultural and subcultural perspectives is too much to do here, or even within the longer essays below. Instead, I shall try my hand at a couple of detailed examples to give a sense of the range of possibilities, beginning with Ukraine.

Interaction is strikingly depicted in a 1987 documentary called *Tomorrow Is a Holiday*, an intense, bleak, oppositional film that details the horrors of life on a large, successful poultry farm, centering on the privations suffered by the women workers and mothers of the twenty-five hundred factory families: little or no hot water, laundry facilities, recreation spaces, cultural events, free time to tend to children, and so on. Music features frequently in this eighteen-minute epic, which shows a visiting music teacher training a chorus to sing a stock supercultural song, in Russian, exhorting them to bellow the refrain, *vpered, vpered, vpered!* ("forward, forward, forward!"). In contrast, the filmmaker includes the women's own habit of forming a sisterhood of singers to do Ukrainian folksongs. A spokeswoman says that their informal song group keeps them from crying or cursing, but has been the target of control by the authorities. The final sequence shows a dismal May Day parade with the triumphant supercultural song ringing out despite the women's well-articulated scorn of holiday celebrations.

Musically, *Tomorrow Is a Holiday* juxtaposes what are usually called "official" and "unofficial" cultures in so-called socialist countries, meaning anything the superculture dishes out as opposed to everything ordinary people or gifted artists produce that is oppositional or alternative. Here, the folksong, once a staple of a peasant superculture, has become a standby of resistance for the oppressed women of the chicken factory as superculture and subculture clash. To see this sort of interaction as part of a larger pattern, let me play it off against what I saw in 1990, also in Ukraine, as part of a Smithsonian Institution delegation to the Second International Folk Festival, an event sponsored by the Soviet Ministry of Culture in Kiev.

Two local supercultures were involved: the federal bureaucracy and the local Ukrainian organizers. The aim was to spotlight troupes from abroad as well as to showcase the entire range of Soviet peoples, from minority groups within the Russian Republic (Siberian, Caucasian, and others), through sample ensembles from the other republics, down to all the regions of Ukraine itself. This program was done by staging (1) a parade down the main street of Kiev; (2) a file-by of troupes in a big soccer stadium, and (3) a second parade, this time with elaborate floats, stereotypes on wheels. The Smithsonian group protested this regimented approach to folklore presentation, so far removed from the American notion of a folklore festival. The Moscow bureaucrats tried to distance themselves by passing the buck to the Ukrainian organizers, showing a slippage among supercultures that had become increasingly the norm in the USSR. Meanwhile, the entire operation was under the umbrella of yet another superculture, one with intercultural implications—a branch of UNESCO that oversees festivals, headed by a Frenchman who kept broadcasting greetings to the crowd.

So much for the framework; now to the content, of which there was very little. With only two exceptions, each troupe was costumed in standard uniforms meant to signify a particular regional or ethnic subculture, and each performed characteristic items. The standouts were the Americans, a deliberately diverse and relaxed group (a New Orleans black funeral band, Tex-Mex *conjunto* players, bluegrass musicians, Hawaiian ritual singers and dancers, tap dancers), and the Latvians. The latter demonstrated their distance from the various supercultures by dressing mostly in street clothes, featuring members from at least three generations, and performing in an amateur, unpolished style.

This disregard of etiquette by these two national troupes served as an exception that proved the rule of regularity, underscoring just how firmly entrenched the basic interaction pattern really was. Yet each conformed to its own supercultural dictates, the Americans to the doctrine of informal cultural pluralism, the Latvian group to an emerging consensus of national sovereignty, part of which demanded uncoupling from the Soviet mainstream notion of how to "do" folklore. The actual membership of the troupe probably represented a subcultural version of this new Latvian superculture. Only patient research could have ferreted out the counterpart meanings of each ensemble, from the Cuban pirate costumes through the Siberian shaman drums. What would probably have emerged would have been a nuanced aesthetic of presentation whose implications were constantly in negotiation between a number of supercultures and a variety of subcultures.

Beyond this battle of facades lies the question of what the folk music/dance presented at the festival really represented. The local Ukrainian case will suffice for present purposes. In the context of Kiev that week in May 1990, the International Folk Festival was just part of a street celebration called "Kiev Day," which included not only the visiting and local "official" troupes but also rural singers imported from nearby villages. The same musical styles were thus presented in two formats: large platforms blasted out standardized, amplified ensembles, and informal singing circles roamed the streets. It was possible to see small knots of Kievans singing along with the villagers just beyond the range of the loudspeakers. While both versions of the Ukrainian folk song represent the superculture in action, the infectious sense of subculture in the spontaneous sidewalk singers was missing from the staged ensembles. The odd part about folklore in this Ukrainian example is that it can serve as both official and unofficial cultures simultaneously, showing that a war of ideoscapes can take place on a single city street with both sides using different varieties of the same cultural weapons within the liminal context of a festival.

The foregoing examples from Ukraine show the complexity of superculture-subculture interaction and point up the importance of ritual moments like holiday celebrations and parades as focal points for cultural confrontation. An anomalous parade from the post-Soviet period marks off the opposite end of the spectrum—the essential meaninglessness of the 1992 Moscow Saint Patrick Day's parade, organized by Irish merchants. A parade without a subculture, an intercultural business gesture, provides the opposite extreme to the charged cultural atmosphere of Kiev.

An American example might better showcase the usefulness of comparative analysis; it comes from Jo Anne Schneider's (1990) description of Polish and Puerto Rican parades in Philadelphia. Kiev and Philadelphia both offer opportunities for local subcultures to display their identity publicly under state-sanctioned auspices, and both celebrate and downplay internal differences within the group, with music being a standardized referent for ethnicity. The superculture's insistence that all groups are equal and, in a sense, identical appears in both venues. For the Soviet scene, it is the relentless, literal uniform-ity of costume that is most striking, for America, the pervasive rhetoric announced by a television reporter: "Everybody is Polish today." Schneider says that Philadelphia's view of "ethnos as the basic unchanging foundation of self" overrides "differences in class, time, and experience" (50), a perspective shared by Kiev.

Glancing back and forth between the two cities shows both similarities and differences. The absence or presence of commodification presented a major distinction. No T-shirts, buttons, or bumper stickers were sold in Kiev. In Philadelphia, not only was commercialism present, it structured the entire event: "The parades last approximately two hours, including commercials . . . the televised version adds theme music" (35). One participant explained: "It used to be that the parade started around one-ish, give or take an hour. And now we realize that we're going to be on television, so it's caused us to be more organized.'" This industrial takeover was, however, nuanced by the triangular relationship between television, the city, and ethnic organizations. As usual, there was both complicity and competition between the wings of the superculture, and, as is often the case, an internal hegemony of subcultural leaders made the game three-cornered: "collusion and contradiction are everywhere evident, especially in speech and symbols" (52).

Here the Kiev-Philadelphia similarities surface once again. The small knots of festival-goers singing along heartily with visiting villagers showed contradictions in the official ideology of the Soviet festival, just as the cracks showed through the patched-together solidarity of Poles or Puerto Ricans in the Philadelphia parade. The hints of conflict between Moscow (read "Russian") and Kiev ("national Ukrainian") interests in the Soviet celebration displayed a tension that was not just administrative—feuding among levels of the superculture—but ethnic, just as the absence of the black mayor of Philadelphia in the Polish parade revealed strong rifts among American subcultures. So, leaving aside important issues of mythology based partly on the differences between a society of immigrants and an empire-based confederation, the public interaction of micromusics and the mainstream suggests considerable overlap.

The American parade behavior only hints at the complexity of boundary maintenance, pride, and upward social mobility, tightly intertwined factors that seem present at nearly all subculture musical events that draw a mainstream audience. Su Zheng's (1990) work in New York's Chinatown provides a helpful example. The Chinese Music Ensemble of New York performs in two venues: downtown in Chinatown for an in-group audience and uptown in standard concert halls for a general public. The program notes for a downtown community concert explain that the event is meant to "help Asian-Americans to be conscious of their cultural heritage and come to a better understanding of it," whereas uptown, the point is to "introduce Chinese music to, and share its wealth with the American public" (26). As a backdrop, an American ideology of tolerance and toleration, pluralism, and upward mobility informs the thinking of everyone involved.

Similar notions appear in most Western liberal democracies. In Britain, the situation of one particular group of South Asian musicians has been deeply shaped by this outlook. According to Baily (1990:164), "In the Indian caste system . . . the Khalifas had a low rank as hereditary musicians. In Britain they live in a society where higher value is placed on music. . . . In the British context the Khalifas are an upwardly mobile community whose members may realize that the profession of musician is unlikely to match other available professions in terms of income and security, but still they feel an attachment to music-making." This situation allows the Khalifas to have their cultural cake and eat it too, and provides a niche for Baily's interlocutor, Ghulam.

Ghulam has a particular history and an individual outlook. Under the conditions of British life, he has been able to reconcile orthodox Islam's condemnation of music by accepting a Western stress on the value of the arts and of personal choice. Hegemony begins at home, with the penetration of ideology as a part of every citizen's inner life. This discussion brings us to *superculture-individual* relations. I can only skim this huge topic, but I would like to point out its power.

Let me start with an everyday example. Perhaps most people in Euro-American societies have a private collection of recordings, expressing the much-vaunted individualism of Western man/woman/child. Bourdieu (1984) has shown us that these choices may produce predictable curves on the graph of socioeconomic realities. Yet his standardized categories allow for little flexibility in terms of personal passion, location in an ethnic subculture, or shifts due to, say, aging. Fiske (1989), on the other hand, is quite eager to show consumer choices as productive "poaching" on the territory of hegemony, as not-so-passive buyers produce meanings from canned popular culture products. Writers on youth subcultures (notably Hebdige 1979) look for the "alternative" and "oppositional" nature of musical activity. Yet they come no closer than Bourdieu to the truly idiosyncratic nature of personal music-making, buying habits, and listening choices. Koskoff (1982) has tried to systematize the very odd networks that help to create personal repertoires, but even she is forced to simplify to create a readable diagram.

This happens because people are often driven by a mixture of memory and desire in their choice of musics, which swings closer to Barthes's passionate *jouissance* than to any set of predictable strategies or methodical mapping. The superculture turns out canned songs as it turns out coffee cans, and in neither case is it clear what the consumer will do with the product. We can no sooner imagine all the uses the average citizen might find for a song than we can imagine what he or she might do with an empty coffee can. This notion of song as free-floating commodity is sometimes touted as being new, or even postmodern, but it is as old as the industry, which I would date to the widespread circulation of lithographed sheet music in the early nineteenth century. If only through the commonplace practice of parody, we know that people were working hard at producing meanings from packaged musical texts long ago.

I would like to take a historic example to point out continuities in this individualization of superculture materials. In 1920, Henryk Rubinlicht, a worldly Warsaw Jew, parodied the text of Schubert's classic song *Staendchen* ("Serenade") as a farewell to his girlfriend on the eve of his departure for the Polish army. His description of that evening is suffused with a lyric romanticism that is quite suitable to the aura of the original song, though it is selectively used: Rubinlicht imposes his own text on Schubert's melody to capture the mood of the moment. His family was rather offbeat in being both middle-class and strongly drawn to the raffish world of the Polish and Yiddish theater scenes. The supercultural components of this tale include exposure to and appropriation of a Schubert song, preference for Polish over Yiddish culture, and orientation to urban entertainment genres.

Let us compare the Rubinlicht "Serenade" to another version of the same song by a second Eastern European Jew, a much less educated woman named Lifsha Schaechter Widman, who grew up at the turn of the century in a remote Bukovina town, within Austria-Hungary but literally across the bridge from Russia. In her rendition, Widman modifies the melodic structure of the song to shape it like her familiar, beloved Yiddish folksongs, changing Schubert's through-composed form into a strophic song based on a quatrain. Unlike Rubinlicht, she keeps the original German text, albeit with a strong Yiddish accent. Widman learned the song either from her one year of formal schooling or from an aunt who had lived in Vienna. Superculture here is a combination of institutional and oral transmission of official culture, but of a very shallow and transient type, a personal choice to graft a bit of hegemony onto her strongly rooted subcultural stock.

Rubinlicht and Widman, many miles apart, belonged to the same Central European superculture, though in radically different lands and ways. The persistence of a single song across these gaps testifies to the strength of musical hegemony. The two creative singers also belonged to the same ethnic-religious subculture. Yet they brought highly charged, different sensibilities to bear on the same canonical item as a result of not only place, time, background, and circumstance, but also temperament. Widman liked to sing Ukrainian songs, as well as an Irving Berlin item from one of her American periods (she emigrated twice), showing her willingness to learn from more than one superculture.

How are we to read these varied responses: as "poaching," "oppositional," "alternative," or merely idiosyncratically creative? In a way, the Schubert "Serenade" is like one of those superculture photographs Barthes discusses in *Camera Lucida* (1981), where he distinguishes the informative cultural data—the *studium*—from the striking detail that catches the imagination—the *punctum*, which varies from observer to observer. For Rubinlicht, the notion of a serenade and the attractive tune captured his view of the song. Widman focused on a part of the melody she could interpret in her individual way. The space between the hegemonic drive and the individual's imagined world is more than a workroom for the *bricoleur*. It is a meeting place of the overdetermined and the accidental. The resulting union is unpredictable. At best, we read tentative regularities into the outcome; these could only be of the most general sort in the Schubert/Jewish example. At worst, we tease out teleologies, find examples to prove our theories.

Music is at once an everyday activity, an industrial commodity, a flag of resistance, a personal world, and a deeply symbolic, emotional grounding for people in every class and cranny the superculture offers. Bourdieu (1984:19) suggests a reason: music "says nothing and has nothing to say . . . music represents the most radical and most absolute form of the negation of the world, and especially the social world, which the bourgeois ethos tends to demand of all forms of art." Ethnomusicology argues otherwise: it is not that music has nothing to say, but that it allows everyone to say what he or she wants. It is not because music negates the world, but because it embodies any number of imagined worlds that people turn to music as a core form of expression.

There are so many types of interactions in the highly articulated, media-dominated societies under review here that a sample of interaction patterns is all I can manage; raising a few additional considerations here may suggest just how many angles of vision are needed.

Interaction among subcultures is rarely the object of scholarly study (for exceptions, see Leary 1984; Slobin and Spottswood 1984), yet at the local level, it may be a force to reckon with as groups cooperate or compete for attention and dollars. Subcultures carry on constant conversations among themselves, creating a musical dialectic that both parallels and is affected by superculture-subculture interaction.

Interaction within subcultures, the productive intramural—often internecine—play among factions is one of the last frontiers of ethnomusicology, posing a set of crucial issues about the way people organize their social and aesthetic lives. In my own New England town, a shift in the 1980s from bumper stickers saying "I'm Proud I'm Italian" to "Proud to be Sicilian" told the tale. In the Jewish world, music-making cannot be understood without delving into the very complex internal politics of factions based on place of origin and time of immigration. Such interaction is as apparent in Sweden and France as in the United States, and yet has been noted in only a few studies, such as Schneider (1990) on parades and in one remarkable monograph on the three-continent (Europe, North and South America) multifactional complexity of Canadian Mennonite singing (Klassen 1989).

The growing body of writings on music in American pan-ethnic movements (summarized in Sommers 1991) testifies to the power of fragmentation by demonstrating the enormous efforts made to overcome it, either for internal reasons or because the superculture demands it—the two causes being hard, if not impossible, to separate. Returning to Zheng's New York Chinese example, the fact that the ensemble chose to locate in Chinatown and the fact that its membership is very heterogeneous (in place of origin, generation, class, gender) are connected: basing oneself in the kind of subcultural "home" an ethnic neighborhood represents clarifies and underscores commitment. It also stereotypes the group in the sense that Chinatown is a brand-name commodity for the uptown audience, strengthening the reciprocal relationship between internal and external definitions of self.

For individuals, choosing among micromusical options can be a form of creative identity, though for some people it can be painful, as in the case of the young half-white, half-Yaqui Indian whom Kealiinohomoku (1986:121) cites. This woman decided to "discover" herself "by becoming active in a large urban Indian center on the West coast," where her associates were largely of Sioux origin. "Many of the Sioux do not accept her. They fault her because her heritage is from the 'wrong' tribe, and because she is half-white. Her distress is expressed by periods of rage alternating with periods of deep depression."

Still within subcultures, *local/interculture intersections* can be very important for diasporic groups, as when New York Greek musicians hear what their colleagues and competitors back home are playing. In John Cohen's eloquent film *Pericles in America*, the vintage Epirotic clarinetist Pericles Halkias rails against younger musicians who have lost a sense of local identity, moving to modernized styles that blur older boundaries. The film is one of the few depictions of American micromusics to present the music and musicians both in the United States and "back home" in Europe, to make a point about the way locales fit onto an intercultural map.

Interaction among intercultures goes on among all possible players, as in the case of subcultural crossover musicians who operate at both the diasporic and the international industrial levels. It is very noticeable in the "Hispanic"-American market, from solo superstars (Julio Iglesias) to upwardly mobile local bands (Los Lobos, Miami Sound Machine). The creation of pan-Hispanic cable systems alongside mainstream networks opens up a parallel-track system linked by advertisers, where interculture-hopping can be the norm. The 1988 bilingual release of the film *La Bamba*, a first for Hollywood, is an example of superculture-subculture intersection. Then, with export, the film becomes an intercultural item as well, showing just how complex the powerful concatenation of the finanscape, mediascape, and technoscape can be in the service of tracking and pocketing ethnoscape markets. In the process, certain ideoscapes are fleetingly activated. The curious quality of the particular product called *La Bamba* is that the plot-line portrays exquisitely stereotyped Mexicans/Mexican-Americans in a way that could have been seen as supercultural aggression, but that in this case was usually overlooked in favor of the "positive" aspects of bilingualism and the foregrounding of subculture music. The soundtrack band, Los

Lobos, seemed to gain strength from its association with Hollywood, which was then intensified when it released a strongly in-group album for balance. Linda Ronstadt, the crossover queen, intersected several audiences and markets successfully in 1988 by emphasizing her father's musical lineage, making a Mexican intercultural connection as well as blurring the superculture-subculture boundary.

To my mind, one of the most fascinating examples of a micromusic built to be interactive is modern country music. This musical complex— for it is hardly unitary—operates at all three levels of analysis I've offered here, and moves freely among them both consciously at the point of production and "out there" among its consumers. Part of the image of country music, so well cultivated and even parodied, is its "plain folks" appeal, which operates in two ways. At the level of subculture, there are still local and regional audiences for whom various generational streams of country music offer the reassurance of looking and sounding "down-home." Nationally, for nearly seventy years, this rustic veneer has served as a wedge for the penetration of country music into far-flung rural and urban markets, well documented in the literature on the upper Midwest (Leary 1984, 1987), the Southwest, including the subcultural zones of Cajun and Native American musics, and even northern New England (McHale 1981). These factors have made country music look supercultural in two ways: first, as the overarching, hegemonic system of its original home base in the heartland, and second, as part of the mainstream American consensus, albeit at a lower level of power than pop musics. What impresses me about this musical formation is the ease with which it projects a multiple appeal, finding new formulas for varied audiences in a chameleonlike fashion.

As a condensed example, let me offer a made-for-country-cable music video that I saw in 1990 of Randy Travis singing "Heroes and Friends." Travis's status as a member of the (apparently non-oxymoronic) category of country singers called "new traditionalists" assumes a back-to-basics subcultural approach that is also proclaimed by his plain clothes and no-frills cinematography, showing him simply dressed, perched on a stool in a bare, old-fashioned recording studio, and singing in a pronounced regional dialect. The confessional nature of the song underscores this stance, as Travis relates how as a kid he watched western movies, adopting their stars as his personal heroes. Images of Roy Rogers are regularly interpolated as direct confirmation of his commentary on the steadfastness and reliability of heroes. At the end of the video, Rogers himself appears, first waving to Travis through the glass studio wall, then in a photograph of the two stars side by side, which closes the video. "Heroes and Friends" simultaneously positions Travis as a subcultural consumer of supercultural stardom, and raises him to parity with his chosen hero. Somehow, the ideology of country music makes this gambit believable, seamless, and heartening. The potential crack between "country" and "western," which, have different histories and are not always allied (see Finnegan 1989 for an English example), is elided here; even more, it serves as grounding for the naturalness of Travis's packaging. However, as a product of Hollywood, Roy Rogers is hardly a purely subcultural idol, and the message about heroes and friends is an all-American statement.

As it happens, the next video on the same program reinforced my interest in these strategies of interaction and inclusion that country uses to move between the subcultural and the supercultural. In it, another Travis, last name Tritt, offers a second confessional song about a singer's aesthetic and ideological orientation. The song tells us how Tritt grew up listening to the legends of his generation (the "outlaws," Waylon Jennings and Willie Nelson), then moved on, sensing the responsiveness of his southern audience toward a new rock-based sound that put "some drive in country." Suitably, the video is couched in MTV quick-cut, girl-centered imagery that underscores the song's rhetoric. Grounding himself in a subcultural music genealogy, Tritt reaches out to mainstream visual/musical aesthetics that he claims are what his (still down-home) audience now wants. This positioning both inside and outside the subculture can be read as just another version of the other Travis's dual appeal.

This dance on the edge of two music-cultural spaces was well presented in the 1991 Grammy Awards ceremonies by the Alabama Headhunters. The group came to the stage to accept their award dressed in torn jeans and T-shirts. In a strongly southern-tinged voice, the spokesman first thanked the folks back in Alabama, Arkansas, and Kentucky who "put out their bucks" to support the band in local clubs. So far, the plain-folks stance and the "country" category of the award were in harmony. Then he closed out the speech by saying how great it was to be on the same stage with John Lennon (who had earlier received a posthumous lifetime achievement award), since the Beatles had been the musical point of departure for the group. Ironies abound here in the evocation of Lennon as a now-sainted superculture hero, given the defiantly antihegemonic thrust of much of his work. Interaction of other layers of superculture and alternative/oppositional subcultures pervade this sort of referencing. The moment was reinforced by having Tracy Chapman introduced as a socially conscious singer who could appropriately sing Lennon's "Imagine." Thus a text proposing the possibility of a nonreligious, noncapitalist world was sung in a glittering celebration of commodified music that was punctuated by winner after winner naming God as the first one to thank for his or her success.

Here ends the dance of the -cultures. The reader may be a bit dizzy from this constant changing of viewpoints, angles of vision, and kaleidoscopic swirls of interaction. I have tried to move up and down levels and across multiple planes of analysis not so much to show how the work *should* be done, but how it *might* be imagined. Again, I am more interested in thinking through the process of work than offering a prefabricated mold into which data can cheerfully—or carelessly—be poured. Still, conceptualization has its limits, so it might be helpful to move on to a closer consideration of the way these energies operate at work and play within subcultural life. Readily conceding that I have not yet offered—and do not intend to offer—a final definition of "subculture," I think that the concept will be strong enough to bear the weight of a few examples of micromusics in action, to which we now turn.

PART THREE

❖

SUBCULTURES AT WORK
AND PLAY

❖

CHAPTER FIVE

The Modes and Means of Expression

❖

Having defined the space within which subcultures express themselves, the next step is to look at how they do it. This section is about techniques—musical approaches and materials. Taking a cue from sociolinguistics, I'll talk first about codes, then about strategies. The underlying assumption is one that crept quietly into ethnographic studies and then took over: that people draw on available resources, reshape them for current needs (bricolage), reevaluate, and start over, building a culture day by day, following strategies, adapting to change. I have found this perspective useful in some of my work on Euro-American musics and will summarize the approach here, then look for implications, limitations, and extensions that widen the focus just a bit.

I remain surprised that ethnomusicology has not had more interaction with sociolinguistics, an obvious sister discipline. Although as early as 1974 Dell Hymes (1974:443) thought that "musical terminology will prove a great resource for exploration of speech styles," few ethnomusicologists have returned the favor by noticing that many terms, concepts, and methods from sociolinguistics might stimulate our discussion of music in culture. In the case of studying subcultures, I find the notion of codes and code-switching particularly helpful, since small groups both generate their own distinctive styles and interact with the styles of the superculture. For my purposes, Labov's (1972:134–35) old definition of code-switching as "moving from one consistent set of co-occurring rules to another" will do. Beyond this bald statement lies a well-documented view that "codeswitching is a conversational strategy used to establish, cross, or destroy group boundaries; to create, evoke, or change interpersonal relations" (Gal 1988:247). Particularly important for a focus on subcultural activity is current thinking that a group's language practices "are part of the group's actively constructed and often oppositional response" to the superculture (ibid.:259). Finally, analysis is multidimensional, not situated in just one sphere of culture contact: Heller (1988:269) proposes an approach that is "historical, ethnographic, and multi-level" in terms of varieties of interaction, of individual style, and of community practice.

As Heller's useful anthropological reader on codeswitching shows, many issues remain highly ambiguous and unexplored in this nearly thirty-year-old field of research. But the anthology also illustrates abundantly how well developed and ingenious the available methodologies are, and how much light the results can shed on the interaction between superculture and subculture. It is worth trying to imagine a musical analogue to the notion of codeswitching. To begin with, however, there is the knotty question of what a musical "code" might be. "Style" is an admittedly slippery concept but is intuitively clear, at least in terms of being a set of consistent rules. For present purposes, "style" can stand for the commonplace categories of everyday music, as in the particular mix of repertoire and mode of presentation that we anticipate when we buy an album or go to a concert, or that dance-band musicians offer as their set of musics for hire. A future, more sophisticated sense of musical code might want to evolve more precise terms that would take account of "languages," "dialects," "levels," and "registers"—all of which count as "codes" for sociolinguists. Local understandings must predominate; the term "modern" as a style category makes sense only as the opposite of "polka" for a Connecticut band described below.

As either musical consumers or producers in Euro-America, people are highly sensitive to finely tuned distinctions in style, as I have learned by talking to a range of insiders from undergraduates to professional musicians. In terms of my interests here, it would be hard to find subcultural music-makers who are not aware of supercultural styles, styles of parallel small groups, and of course the many modes of expression of their own micromusical colleagues. The resources that even bathtub singers can draw on are numerous enough: popular, patriotic, seasonal, advertising, and many other materials are on the tip of the tongue. The really problematic question is: Do musicians switch from style to style on purpose? When a jazz musician quotes Beethoven, when a Latino singer mixes English phrases into his Spanish, when an ultra-Orthodox Jewish songwriter sets Hebrew texts to a rock tune, we can hardly imagine that they do so accidentally. It is no easier to determine exactly why, where, and how codeswitching occurs for players and composers than it is for speakers, though I will try my hand at a few examples below.

One more crucial point about music: it's richer in codes than language. True, utterances can be combined with intonation patterns and gestures to add layers of meaning, but even highly expressive speakers can draw on fewer variables than can musicians. A band playing a song can pull together not just text and tune, but timbre, rhythm, and instrumentation for several performers simultaneously in a stratified system I call code-layering, style upon style upon style; it can then shift any number of the variables in the next section to produce a new kaleidoscopic code combination. Analysis becomes a process of untying a musical knot and seeing where all the strings come from before proceeding to the next node in the fabric. Another metaphor would suggest reconstructing the work of the Sunday do-it-yourselfer by taking apart his contraption to figure out what materials he used and how he put them together. You hope the process will illuminate his motives, but you can't really be sure without asking—if he remembers and wants to tell you his secrets.

Let me begin with a clear-cut example of sharp, stark codeswitching. A Jewish-American comedy number of the late 1940s by a talented duo (the Barton Brothers) begins with one brother giving a perfectly standard recitation of Longfellow's hoary all-American poem "The Midnight Ride of Paul Revere," accompanied by a trumpet-and-drum rendition of "The Battle Hymn of the Republic," thus layering patriotic code upon code. The diction and dialect of this first Barton Brother are standard, slightly pompous American English. Suddenly, the nationalistic reverie is broken by a brief silence and a highly dramatic codeswitch to a band playing an Eastern European Jewish dance tune that accompanies the other Barton Brother. The second brother uses a heavy Yiddish intonation and delivers a parody of the "Midnight Ride" ("Paul Rabinowitz," and so on) in a Yiddish full of English lexical intrusions. A short section of this Euro-American mishmash is followed by a break that introduces the return of the all-American Longfellow code. The two components of the performance alternate in unbroken succession until the duo cover the entire poem: musical superculture and subculture alternate in a strictly ordered progression of solo turns. Such "block" codeswitching, particularly the perfect alignment of codes within each section, is rather rare; the incongruity of precise juxtaposition dominates, rather than multitrack overlays.

What did the Barton Brothers have in mind? I could do an elaborate analysis on the basis of long acquaintance with Jewish-American expressive culture, but I will spare the reader here. The point for the present is that codeswitching is of great strategic value as a musical resource, and that it probably implies strong sentiments. Whatever the performers' intent, they had no control over the audience response, so simple ethnography will not provide a full answer; such materials can point in many directions, and they change over. The numerous meanings that the community produces at any one point give rise to ever-new implications as cultural vistas open up. Let's compare the Barton Brothers' use of patriotic material to that in another Jewish-American popular song, back in 1917. In *"Onkel Sem"* ("Uncle Sam"), code-switching is equally dramatic. An opening section in minor with a strong European voice quality for the Yiddish song text explains that, having found a happy home in America, the Jew must be ready to shed his blood for his new fatherland. A short pause separates this style from the conclusion of the song, which consists of (1) the opening bars of "The Star-Spangled Banner," and (2) the closing phrase of George M. Cohan's patriotic song "You're a Grand Old Flag." While *"Onkel Sem"* and "The Midnight Ride" differ widely, if not wildly, in the way they use nationalistic materials, they share common codes and strategies.

Let's give ethnography its due and see what fieldwork can turn up by way of motivation for codeswitching-layering. A 1986 interview with a successful modern religious songwriter in the Jewish tradition (I'll call him David) produced a very clear self-analysis of technique. At the point where we enter the conversation, David and I are discussing the "new" popular religious music, which is a major trend among American Jews:

D.   That's another harmonic distinction of the new music—that lowered leading tone [demonstrates on guitar].
M.S.   Does that come out of rock, you think?
D.   Yeah—no; it don't—it doesn't, it comes out of Jewish music, and it comes out of Israeli music. That's probably to my mind the single most prevalent melodic tendency of Israeli music. Any Israeli song has that lowered leading tone.
M.S.   It's also what the Beatles and other people . . .
D.   . . . You have that in rock too. . . . so my music has that lowered leading tone influence. There's little of that [plays tonic-dominant-tonic progression] because to me, that's ordinary, that's Stephen Foster. . . . Now my new music has gotten a little more—Jewish in character. Because I've assimilated more, and I start to think about what I want to leave here [plays what he calls a "middle period" song, illustrating components]. That's the lyricism—but it has a nice neat pop ending. And here are the "third chords"—jazzy feel. I was pretty happy with that melody.

In David's case, strategy is foregrounded. He is trying to write a personally satisfying song that will catch on with a broad audience. He tunes in to current trends for both reasons: he is a child of his time, and so is his (largely younger) audience. He not only is aware of switching codes, but can identify them for an interviewer, and in doing so makes some motivations clear. The ethnicity of the music needs to be unquestioned, so he identifies the "lowered-seventh chord" as being Israeli rather than rock in origin, while conceding it could be either. For David's style, standard codes include "Israeli," "Mediterranean," "jazz," "pop," "rock," "old-fashioned, Stephen Foster," and a few others (e.g., "Hasidic") that didn't come up in the quoted excerpt. But they are only melodic/harmonic/rhythmic codes: the use of Hebrew sacred texts, with an insistence on "correct accentuation," is a bedrock assumption of all his songs and is non-negotiable; the presumed authenticity is indispensable to validate the songs and the songwriter for socioreligious reasons.

David's case shows that it is possible to untangle the meanings and resonance of musical codes, given articulate musicians, of whom there are many in European/American societies, and to move toward understanding their strategic value. Subcultural musicians keep one eye on their in-group audience and the other on the superculture, looking out for useful codes and successful strategies, while a third, inner eye seeks personal aesthetic satisfaction. No wonder there are so many detours along the path, since all three audiences are restless. Indeed, the musicians' own creations contribute to internal change and outside reevaluation of subcultural life, leading them to further alteration as they adjust to personal, inner, and outer imagined worlds of music, just as the modes and meanings of linguistic resources are in constant motion. A young composer/performer like David can speak of a song being "from my middle period," revealing a strong historical perspective and demonstrating that any current statement about his creative stance could only be provisional.

There may be larger processes at work that are more durable. If we pull back from the microworld of individuals, a bird's-eye view reveals fairly stable ways that the larger subculture tends to work on its musics, a set of basic strategies—of which codeswitching is but one—that may be conscious or intuitive. I think of these as a set of relationships to resources, attitudes toward the huge range of available choices. Some involve responses to the superculture, while others center on decisions about internal repertoires, styles, genres, texts, and contexts. My approach here boils down to a bunch of -tion words to indicate accomplished act-tions. My interest is in trying to be fairly precise about terms without being pedantic, in avoiding overgeneralized, often overdetermined -tions like "acculturation" or "assimilation." Jewish-American examples, where I can best vouch for plausibility, might predominate, but I will throw in others as counterweights and controls.

The first perspective involves the way that subcultures use the superculture's musical materials. This perspective includes several approaches and a vast variety of items, as such interactions lie at the heart of a subculture's definition of itself and its boundaries. Writing or lecturing on this topic, scholars tend to use many words, often very loosely, from the most general, *syncretism*, to rather pointed terms, like the currently fashionable *appropriation*. It might be best to follow the lead of the art historian Michael Baxandall, who utterly condemned the all-too-vague phrase "influenced by" (a term not unknown in ethnomusicological circles), "which I must spend a couple of pages trying to kick just enough out of my road to pass on." Speaking of artist X "influencing" artist Y, he finds the concept "impoverished" because it is richer to "think of Y rather than X as the agent." Translating this view to music, we might make X = the superculture, Y = the subculture, and we might agree with Baxandall that then "the vocabulary is much richer and more attractively diversified":

Draw on, resort to, avail oneself of, appropriate from, have recourse to, adapt, misunderstand, refer to, pick up, take on, engage with, react to, quote, differentiate oneself from, assimilate oneself to, assimilate, align oneself with, copy, address, paraphrase, absorb, make a variation on, revive, continue, remodel, ape, emulate, travesty, parody, extract from, distort, attend to, resist, simplify, reconstitute, elaborate on, develop, face up to, master, subvert, perpetuate, reduce, promote, respond to, transform, tackle . . . —everyone will be able to think of others (Baxandall 1985 : 59).

All of which boils down to: "Responding to circumstances, Y makes an intentional selection from an array of resources in the history of his craft," a response not far from the type of cultural improvisation I have been and will be describing.

One way to handle the terminology of music-cultural processes might be to use as many words as possible, each conveying a rather specialized approach, then to talk about overlaps. Suppose we try out a term I've already used—*domestication*—on music brought into the subculture from the superculture. *Domestication* literally means bringing into the house; it implies the harnessing of something wild, uncontrollable, and putting it to good household use. Playing the dictionary game, we let the Oxford English Dictionary give us both "to attach to home and its duties" and "to tame or bring under control." Many cases of "borrowing" seem to have this thrust, or at least it can be seen as a component of musical transplantation.

Domestication in both OED senses comes very close to the mark in describing the practice of Hasidic Jews in Europe and America when it comes to the use of superculture materials. The charismatic sectarian leaders of Eastern Europe took over non-Jewish materials in which they sensed an imprisoned sacred "spark" that needed to be released. So a Napoleonic march of a passing French army or a banal tune being cranked out by an organ grinder in a dusty town square could be turned into a celebratory, even ecstatic song by nineteenth-century European Hasidim, while in America, pop songs and even advertising jingles (Koskoff 1978), symbols of the impure, dangerous, Gentile secular world, can be turned to good use within the Hasidic spiritual "home."

Let us try a radically different case: a record of an American "Middle Eastern" night-club-style music that features an "orientalized" version of the Beatles song "Yesterday." That song being the most recorded item in musical history, it is hardly surprising that it can be domesticated to do its duty of entertaining. On the record, it acts as a sharp codeswitch from the "homeland" style of the previous track, suggesting the band's complete mastery of its audience's tastes, which span the in-group and the mainstream spheres. The fact that the ensemble subjects "Yesterday" to a rather intense defamiliarization might suggest domestication—the song has certainly been effectively harnessed. Interviews would help fix the performers' intent but would tell us little about consumer reception. How do listeners hear the codeswitch, perceive the playing around with a canonical pop text? Certainly some of them smile, as do most listeners for whom I play the tape; the incongruity of piece and overlaid parody makes people laugh. Is the process at work domestication? borrowing? appropriation? eclecticism? acculturation? assimilation? Americanization? Some words seem more suitable than others for this example, though the multivalent nature of the musical text means that no one term can cover all possible meanings, resonances, nuances. Trying out a large vocabulary, rather than settling on one blanket term for many differing cases, would at least push the analyst to consider the broad range of motivations and receptions a subcultural move can represent.

Let us return to "The Midnight Ride of Paul Revere" in its Yiddish incarnation. Here the disjuncture between superculture and subculture sounds more shocking than the transition from in-group sound to "Yesterday." The original and its parody are segmented and performed in strict alternation with short breaks between units. The Barton Brothers do more violence to the original than does the Middle Eastern band, and the all-American text is not only patriotic, but nearly sacred; their intervention is a musical equivalent to treading on the flag. Perhaps this kind of vehemence might bring the term "appropriation," even "confiscation," into play. Certainly such militant domestication suggests that "home" is a combat zone that mirrors the "Battle Hymn" and the militarism of the Longfellow segments.

If we continue to use the theme of patriotism, Ray Henry's "Bicentennial Polka" might help crack this particular code. The piece opens with a flourish of trumpets and drums in a march beat, suggesting nationalism. A code-switch brings the same instruments into line with the Polish-American polka sound, in which they also feature prominently, over the 2/4 beat common to both polka and march. Henry enters with the following text:

> When I look back into history
> So many long years ago
> In the greatest country ever
> Which I love and do adore.

The opening flourish returns, now confirmed as being patriotic, the polka backup reenters, and the text continues:

> Started right here in New England
> Some two hundred years ago
> With the call of Paul Revere
> Which echoed 'round the world.
>
> Since then she's had her ups and downs
> In peacetime as well as war
> She always has defended
> The freedom of one and all.

Finally:

> And now I would like to thank her
> From the bottom of my heart
> For the freedom and the good life
> That here we all enjoy.

The happy coincidence that trumpets, drums, and a steady 2/4 rhythm characterize both the patriotic and the polka sounds allows Henry to make a statement that is simultaneously of the subculture and the superculture; the result is almost a code "fusion." The situation is underscored by his singing in English instead of introducing the Polish-English code-switching that marks off some polka songs as "ethnic." The fact that Henry's message is being projected from the small stage of a subculture to the large arena of national ideology pushes the listener to define a cultural space for the music, or at least to turn up a term. Certainly a kind of "accommodation" has been reached, and the coziness of the internal-external rapprochement suggests domestication of the patriotic as integral to the expressive home. Far from the Barton Brothers' assaults, here Paul Revere stands firmly on his pedestal, even acquiring the "heard round the world" tag line that belongs to the "shot" fired in an Emerson poem about the first battle of the American Revolution.

The foregoing comparison between two ethnic Paul Reveres—one perhaps confrontational, the other more accommodating—brings to the surface a question latent throughout this book: the oppositional nature of subcultural sounds. Writers on this topic vary widely. The cultural theorist George Lipsitz, in *Time Passages* (1990), describes the complex, inter-ethnic, struggling world of Los Angeles Chicano music-makers, and chooses to see the oppositional as subtext for a wide variety of texts, contexts, and personal choices by musicians. He argues that the attempts of Chicano rockers to mainstream their music "by linking up with other oppositional cultures reflect their struggle to assemble a 'historical bloc' capable of challenging the ideological hegemony of Anglo cultural domination" (152). The music theorist Don Randel, writing about the *salsa* star Ruben Blades, takes a somewhat different tack (1991). Randel wants to downplay the possibly negative implica-tions of the word "crossover" commonly applied to Blades, whom he sees as "not crossing over *to* a new audience so much as he is crossing over *with* a new audience whose culture is profoundly Hispanic but in-creasingly imbued with Anglo culture and energized by its very own political and economic aspirations" (31). It would be easy for me to agree or disagree with either Lipsitz's or Randel's assessments of Latino musicians, including their seemingly varying attitudes about opposi-tionality in subcultural music. Though well informed, neither state-ment is based on extensive fieldwork data among audiences. Ethnomusi-cology's lack of serious reception studies is particularly telling when we approach ideology.

My own preference for the moment is to look for methodological possibilities. To return to the two Paul Reveres—Polish- and Jewish-American—I would like to raise the question of codeswitching once again, viewed from sociolinguistics. In a closely argued, empirically based study much more typical of that discipline than of ethnomusi-cology, Shana Poplack (1988) discusses contrasting patterns of code-switching in two communities, Puerto Ricans in New York and French-Canadians in Ottawa-Hull, Ontario. The contrasts are many. For example, the Puerto Rican view codeswitching as "emblematic of their dual identity, and smooth, skilled switching is the domain of highly flu-ent bilinguals," whereas for the French-Canadians, "highlighting, flag-ging, or otherwise calling attention to the switch" is important. Poplack does not venture far toward telling us *why* these groups act differently, but cautions that "the striking contrasts . . . do not augur well for any simple deterministic view of bilingual behavior" (Poplack 1988:237–38). She can draw on seventeen hundred examples of codeswitching per group, can define her codes with considerable precision, and can determine issues like grammaticality, to name just three tools in her analytical workshop, none of which are available for music (at least, I know of no ethnomusicological study that can draw upon so extensive and precise a database). Yet the closer she scrutinizes the scene, the more wary she is of drawing comfortable conclusions.

However, such care is itself a source of comfort. The questions become ever more acutely posed, the troublesome issues more strongly spotlighted. For example, Poplack spends some anxious moments worrying about how to tell loanwords from codeswitches, before deciding that there may not be any a priori way of doing so. She warns: " 'Momentary' borrowing has to be distinguished from incomplete acquisition and language loss [and] all of these phenomena should be distinguished from speech errors which involve elements of both languages and which may be properly considered 'interference.' " This caution leads to the payoff statement that "what appears to be the same phenomenon may have a different status from one bilingual community to another" (239). So elaborate precision in one field site, with a similarly rigorous follow-up elsewhere, leads to an exquisite appreciation of the highly situated nature of all language use and a helpful skepticism about terminology.

We have a long way to go in music studies to reach such a plateau; most of our ethnographic studies are still one-shot surveys or broad historical overviews. It is hard to imagine a fieldwork project that would compile seventeen hundred examples of musical codeswitching in one small community. My hunch is that if we *did* do such research, we probably would end up in the same place. Separating patterned use from error and borrowing from codeswitching, and extending the findings to comparisons between communities would certainly be just as complicated, but would also be very rewarding in what we might learn about how micromusics work—and play, since both are involved here.

Let me return to what we can attempt with the materials at hand. So far I have stayed close to codeswitching or simple layering by language substitution, but many subcultural musics engage in complex layering, piling code upon code. Take, for example, the case of Ukrainian-Canadian country-western music, ably described by Klymasz (1972) in one of the earliest incisive accounts of a North American subcultural style. Pick up any record: a band can take a standard American country song like "Please Release Me," translate the lyrics into Ukrainian and sing them with a nonstandard timbre, add at least one European backup instrument like the cimbalom, shift the rhythmic emphasis, and so on, creating a hybrid genre. We might begin to reach for -tions like "reconfiguration" or "recontextualization" to characterize the shifting, kaleidoscopic patterns of codes that subcultures can create by modifying superculture musical materials, a sort of "customization" of assembly-line products.

Yet a great deal of the subculture's musical energy goes into working over its *own* music in a process I call "reevaluation." Over time, new perspectives cause a reordering of group priorities, a changed understanding of what is "authentic," what represents "us" best to outsiders, what sells best to a new generation of listeners, or what is now "ours" that once was "theirs." Such shifts often accompany significant social change in the superculture or a particular historical moment in the life of the subculture.

Recent Jewish-American musical trends are exemplary here. Somewhere around 1960 the Jews stopped being considered a "minority group" and started figuring as unmarked members of the American majority from the point of view of bureaucrats, courts, and college administrators. This moment coincided with a general rise in comfort as part of postwar suburbanization and affluence. It is perhaps not surprising then, that from the 1960s on, the internal diversity, even playfulness, of in-group music-making has increased sharply. Take, for example, two performances of a Yiddish folksong, *"Di mame iz gegangn"* ("Mama Went to Market") one from the late 1950s and the other from the mid 1980s. The first, by Theodore Bikel, a Hollywood actor-cum-folksinger, comes from his record of Yiddish folksong favorites that seemed to be in every Jewish home at the time. The format and delivery of the song stick to the mainstream folk-revival sound of the period: steady tempo, clean melodic and instrumental lines, guitar backup, precise diction that sounds slightly distanced from a European base. The second version, by the New York *klezmer* band Kapelye (even the Yiddish-English term *"klezmer* band" for such ensembles did not exist until the late 1970s) offers a striking contrast in every parameter of performance. The backup band is diverse, from tuba to banjo, and often raucous. The tempo shifts from opening recititative style, with instrumental interjections, to accelerating, then bracing, breakdown speed. The singer, Michael Alpert has a broadly European Yiddish. A street or dance-prone audience seems envisioned, far from the suburban living-room setting the Bikel version conjures up.

As much as I dislike psychologizing a subculture, it is hard for me not to believe that this sort of unbuttoned ethnic music-making by young Jewish-Americans is tied to the fact that for Jews, ethnic boundaries are now erected more from the inside out than from the outside in. You don't have to be as careful with your daily life if no one is peering in the window. You might dust off some skeletons in the closet, or reconsider your embarrassment at the way your old relatives behave, perhaps viewing them as interesting eccentrics—or even as role models.

A more dramatic internal musical shift than "*Di mame*" is provided by the recent Hasidic song boom among non-Hasidic American Jews. A word of explanation is in order. For decades, the garb and folkways of the ultra-Orthodox, sectarian Hasidim were a subject of ridicule or scorn by mainstream Jewish-Americans. The idea that such patently foreign, insistently Yiddish-speaking insular Jews could represent a rapidly suburbanizing, increasingly affluent minority group would have made no sense at all in 1940, or even 1960. Yet by 1980 the Hasidim were seen as the authentic, quintessential Jews, and their influence over Jewish-American culture has been growing at a rapid rate although they constitute only a small percentage of the ethnic group. Hasidic tunes have found their way into the worship services of many congregations and sell very well, prompting non-Hasidic composers to imitate the style to catch the wave of popularity. The Hasidim have not changed their dress, language, or habits, but they occupy a new cultural space. Even the *New York Times* has featured a Hasidic apartment in its prestigious front-page "Living" section slot.

This sort of "reevaluation" is precisely what I have in mind. A shift in outlook causes one to stop and reconsider even deeply felt views about the validity of elements of one's own subculture. Since ethnicity of the sort at work here is symbolic and not socially serious in terms of a person's status in the superculture, why not play with cultural forms? After all, there are expressive rewards. Congregants find weekly services much more enjoyable when they can sing catchy, rhythmic Hasidic tunes and even clap their hands rather than sit back and listen to the authority figures—rabbi and cantor—run the show. For young people, this sort of participatory appeal is particularly strong. Curiously, it comes at some cost to the earlier, powerful appeal of Israeli music. A de-emphasized reliance on Israel as an emotional focus may be the backdrop to this decline in musical influence. Complicating the picture is the diasporic network of Hasidic communities and their imitators, which sees American musicians populating Israeli scenes while the Israel-based Hasidic Song Festival sells out in New York.

This brief foray into the internal life of a single subculture shows just how complex and intense even small-scale community musical life can be in the large multigroup nation-states under discussion. It also displays the cyclical life of codes, which flicker in and out of communal consciousness. Once parodied mercilessly on the Yiddish stage in the immigrant era (1880s–1920s) and beyond, the stylized Hasidic codes are having their day at the forefront of Jewish-American expressive culture. The penetration of this particular code complex into the superculture needs to be mentioned: the musical traffic flows in both directions. In building *Fiddler on the Roof*, its creative team turned to Hasidic celebrations as a source of material for dance and to the old, unaccompanied, meditative *nign* tune as an inspiration for the ethnic tinge that the Broadway sound needed to set off the show—just listen to Tevya's "yob-a-dob-a . . ." in "If I Were a Rich Man" (for a detailed account, see Altman and Kaufman 1971). Because the creators of *Fiddler* were Jewish, the construction of this Broadway landmark proceeded from an internal discussion of how subcultural codes and messages might successfully be built into the supercultural space. In general, I think the reciprocal relationship between superculture and subculture has been downplayed in our enthusiasm for locating hegemony.

I have demonstrated very few tools of the analyst's workshop in this section, partly to keep the discussion condensed and partly because I have tried out illustrations elsewhere (e.g., Slobin 1988 on iconography). I have also not done much cross-referencing of concepts. For example, the trumphal spread of *Fiddler on the Roof* around the world as a classic American musical brings in the interculture, while the whole process involves shifting of visibility levels, from local to regional to transregional. A working knowledge of intra-subcultural music-making at the smallest levels of technique is not just of local interest culturally or analytically, since the various planes and levels are continuously cross-cutting.

Looking at the modes and means of micromusical work and play cannot be a self-sufficient approach, even within the expressive life of a subculture, for at any point in a musical system, techniques exist only as tools on the workbench until the *bricoleur* arrives to begin tinkering. The embodiment of trends and tropes happens in performance, where the actors arrange themselves into easily identifiable groups. Although the ensemble has become increasingly standard as a unit of analysis for places like Africa, for Euro-America, the work has only recently begun, and needs the kind of thinking-through I hope the next chapter will provide.

CHAPTER SIX

Ensembles—Banding versus Bonding

❖

Ensembles define everyday music-making in Euro-American life as nothing else can. As collectives, they stand for individuals bonded by belonging, or for the whole group in microcosm. For outsiders—for the superculture in general—ensembles often *are* the micromusic, since they are what appear at display events like parades, folk festivals, night clubs, and concert halls. For my purposes, they come in two types: *bands*, that is, performing units of professional or semiprofessional musicians that play for the pleasure of paying customers, and *affinity groups*, charmed circles of like-minded music-makers drawn magnetically to a certain genre that creates strong expressive bonding. With these two varieties of ensembles, we can further map the subcultural space between individual soundworlds and the products of the superculture.

Bands are particularly adept at placing themselves anywhere in this territory: at the center of the subculture as focal flashpoint, on the margins as musical adventurers, or even abroad, posted as ambassadors to the superculture. Often they position themselves on the fence, the way a band at a Hasidic wedding plays on the wall between the male and the female dancers, both sides sharing the acoustic space but doing different steps, or in the manner of Gypsy ensembles serving as similarly nongendered, almost nonhuman dance-makers at a wedding in Greece (Cowan 1990). Any subcultural ensemble might perform for several audiences (e.g., various generations) at a single event or on alternate nights for different crowds, making sure to please them all. Affinity groups, however, locate themselves at a determined point and may even build walls around their musical strongholds. They serve as nuclei for the free-floating units of our social atmosphere, points of orientation for weary travelers looking for a cultural home. A look at some selected small musical groupings can stand in for the grand survey we so badly need.

I'll start with bands, collectives that play for a crowd that is either listening/eating or dancing. Bands are flexible, since we are dealing here with specialists who have put a great deal of time and energy into approaching a certain ideal of musical sound. Whose ideal that might be is what is under discussion—their own, reflexive imagined world, or that of an audience of listeners or dancers who are paying for the pleasure of commanding a performance. Audience-pleasing is certainly a central concern.

Let me begin with the eloquent testimony of Lawrence Welk, an extraordinarily successful American band leader, on the universality of one basic cultural demand:

> I found out all over again that people everywhere who liked to dance had one thing in common, whether they danced in an empty garage in Coldwater, Kansas, or in the most ornate ballroom in the country. They wanted music with a good strong rhythmic beat and a tune they recognized (Welk 1971:162).

Oddly enough, ethnomusicology has not produced a general account of the formation, hiring, and reception of the dance band, although it is a staple of societies around the globe. My own experience in Afghanistan would back up Lawrence Welk's opinion; looked at in such basic terms, the strategies of band-leading have little to do with geography. Nor does the basic relationship of performer to audience in such situations have much to do with a folk-popular divide, or even a superculture-subculture gulf. In Welk's case, the basic performer-audience contract varied little from the days when he toured small-town North Dakota as a German-American accordionist to his heady heyday as a bandleader in metropolitan hotels. His enormous success on television shows that it is possible to transfer a style from the danced to the watched modes. Conversely, the neo-*klezmer* movement of 1970s–80s Jewish dance music quickly moved from concert format to audience participation, turning a ticket-paying crowd into a facsimile of wedding guests.

What attract the analyst here are the strategies, the ways to win over whatever audience is at hand, well observed for the Moroccan scene by Schuyler (1984), but sparsely described for Euro-America. This is commercial music, and the object is to keep the jobs coming in week after week, season after season. Precisely because the musical resources are so rich in our times, musicians can find the right combination for a particular crowd. So the distinctions between superculture and subculture bands might not be all that great at the level of crowd-pleasing.

Ray Henry, a durable southern New England polka-band leader, has stayed within micromusic bounds, unlike the roughly contemporary Lawrence Welk, but his commentary is not far in spirit from Welk's:

I would say there's two types of musicians: there's a good one and there's the smart one. You have to adapt yourself quickly. You play your own stuff and you watch them, and in no more than half an hour, you're going to play *their* way. If you see they're dancing fast, you better play fast, and if they like a lot of polkas, you better play a lot of polkas. That's what it's all about. (Spalding 1986:71)

Bruce MacLeod's 1979 dissertation, aptly titled "Music for All Occasions," is still the only study I know of the everyday Euro-American big-city "club-date" musician's life. Although the New York scene he describes has drastically shrunk because of the incursions of recorded sound for private parties, his study holds up very well as a general description of the demands on the working live musician who provides expressive marking for celebrations, whether corporate/political or personal/life-cycle. The scene can be what musicians call "a lobster in the woods" (private mansion) or a catering hall near the freeway, and the musicians can be MacLeod's all-purpose members of New York's Local 802 of the American Federation of Musicians or an unregistered band fresh off a plane from Greece who will head back to Europe in a couple of weeks. All show that while "he who pays the piper calls the tune," the payment circumscribes the musician more than the customer. The important point here is how viewing things from the perspective of band life illuminates the other planes of our discussion of micromusical life. An excellent case in point comes from Ruth Glasser's (1990) study of New York's Puerto Rican musicians in the 1920s and 1930s. By zooming in on the professional musicians of a particular "ethnic group," Glasser broadens rather than narrows the focus of analysis, which includes several key issues:

Superculture interaction. Like recent work on Jewish musicians of this period (Slobin and Spottswood 1984), Glasser's research shows that it is impossible to understand even the most "in-group" of music-making without factoring in the demands of industry: "the influence of large American record companies on the popularization and even the formation of various genres of Latin music cannot be overstated" (Glasser 1990:70). Meanwhile the superculturally produced and media-packaged lumping together of a wide variety of groups as "Latins" led Puerto Rican bands to become "complicit in their stereotyping as interchangeable Latins by adopting Mexican, Argentine, or Cuban musical images and forms" (ibid.).

Intercultural implications. The commercial connection meant that New York musicians colonized their compatriots. Glasser says that "the companies also counted on the versatility of their musicians to efficiently provide records for a large portion of Latin America." At the same time, diasporic intercultural linkages paralleled those of industry, as, say, Puerto Rican bandleader Rafael Hernandez "returned from years in Cuba" and brought in new styles (69).

Inter-subcultural dealings. Much of Glasser's short article details the way Puerto Rican band members interacted with both their "Latin" cousins and African-American ensembles, as in Juan Tizol joining Duke Ellington's band, or less celebrated players finding work in black reviews during the Harlem Renaissance. Important here is that these band members did not switch "loyalties" out of desperation, but simply relied on the versatility they had had to begin with, back in Puerto Rico, working in municipal bands. Here again the Puerto Rican experience jibes with that of immigrant Eastern European Jewish bands or Punjabi musicians in Britain, weaned on eclecticism in their homeland and able to turn it to advantage in club or recording dates in the West.

Intra-subcultural variety. Every subculture, each micromusic, is a world unto itself. The variety of homeland repertoires just mentioned is a starting point. Puerto Rican casinos, for example, had included "foxtrots, two-steps, one-steps, mazurkas, and waltzes . . . since at least the early twentieth century" and had carried out a "long-time love affair with the Argentine *tango*" (65). There are always class differences, such as those Peña carefully spells out for Texas-Mexicans, which hold true equally for Caribbean musical life. Glasser sums up the situation among New York's early Puerto Rican bands this way: "These musicians evade the archetypal historical image of an ethnic population's culture crumbling and succumbing to 'American' forms, instead suggesting endlessly creative combinations and recombinations of a variety of ethnic musics" (69). Far from presenting the image of a constrained ghetto community, Glasser offers the picture of a lively microworld in which "the smallness and newness of the Puerto Rican community did not mean that either musicians or audience members retreated to some sort of geographically and culturally cohesive world."

Glasser's historical perspective is important, since so often current American subcultural expressions are portrayed as a novel departure, as post-1960s shifts from established patterns. Our viewpoint is all too limited by the lack of solid surveys of a large number of earlier micromusics. At this point, it might help to turn to bands of older, Euro-American immigrant populations to see how their rather more attenuated ties to the past work themselves out on the dance floor.

Mary Spalding (1986) spent considerable time with the Irene Olszewski Orchestra of the New Britain/Hartford (Connecticut) area, and this Polish group can provide some points of orientation. The band plays two kinds of "jobs"—"polka" and "modern" (mainstream). I will focus just on the former here, as I'm more concerned at the moment with in-group habits than with mainstream aesthetics. Still, even a polka job in a polka hall may not be performed for an all-Polish audience, for non-Polish spouses or polka-job habitués may also need to be brought into the spirit of the evening; any notion of "interiority" of subcultural expression has to be strongly qualified. Another complicating variable is the type of Pole in the crowd, since two periods of immigration are represented in Connecticut: Polish-Americans who are descended from the great wave of the early twentieth century, and relative or complete newcomers, subdivided into pre- and post-Solidarity periods. A band member explains the difference in taste while describing a job with "pre-dominantly Polish immigrants . . . a lot of them were not able to speak English. Well, they had a whole different idea of what a polka should be like. They like it fast! They're more for waltzes as opposed to polkas and, typically, they're big on tangos" (47). There is a further constraint: polka-job crowds are older than modern-job crowds. They are "over forty" and have rather fixed expectations, which extend from wanting the band to look "tailored and professional" to playing many audience requests.

Faced with an urgent need to please, Olszewski must also respond to another professional drive: the commercial imperative of being original, memorable. She opens with one of the band's own tunes: "It's something they haven't heard before unless they've heard us. I like to start by saying we're different, we're unique. I always try to establish our identity right from the start" (53). This type of originality is one of the distinguishing marks of the micromusic band as opposed to its main-stream counterpart. MacLeod's New York club-date musicians may play ethnic numbers for subcultural events like Italian weddings and Jewish bar mitzvahs, but they have no real need to prove themselves as "origi-nal"; if anything, they downplay distinctiveness in favor of reliability. While the Olszewski Orchestra can hardly afford to play all their own material, they do need to come up with something that will make them stand out from a crowded micromusical marketplace, where the gigs are few and the stakes are low.

After the opening "signature" tune, the bandleader provides a "road map" for the evening through announcements to the audience. Then she simultaneously leads them through a set of tunes that she hopes will get them happy and follows the crowd, as it interrupts with requests. Many items played are polka standards, "songs that have been recorded by thousands of bands over the years with thousands of different arrangements. They've probably been played in every club in the country . . . they've endured where others haven't," says Irene Olszewski (57). As in all such canonical dance-tune repertoires, from jazz through Broadway-based "society"-band books, standards provide musicians with butter on both sides of their bread: they show off the group as being reliable and knowledgeable while they showcase virtuosity by allowing for new arrangments of old standbys—within limits. Bands can "add their own touch to it to sound a little different . . . as long as you don't change it too much where people don't recognize it," says Joe Olszewski (58). His statement helps draw a line between the rules of dance-band musi-cians and those of an "art" or "concert" group that can enjoy pushing audience expectations without having to worry about dancers tripping up their partners. After all, it is the dancers who pay the piper, and the musicians have to keep them not only happy but healthy:

After four polkas, you're ready to break down a little bit, and the people are ready to breathe a little bit. Polkas are strenuous: people can have a heart attack dancing the polka. And that's a legitimate sentence because I've seen it hap-pen! . . . Some of it is also physical for us. We might just need a break . . . but it's for the people. We have to really gear first for them. (60)

As in other dance-band contexts, a higher percentage of standards (and heart attacks) signifies an older crowd. Joe explains that "if everyone there were younger—thirty-five and down—I would probably play more recent tunes" (59).

It would seem that factors such as the type of job, the generation of the audience, and the wave of immigration might make gigs predict-able, allowing for safe strategies. Yet surprises are yet another variable. "Hopefully, in the first three songs, you have your audience pegged for the night. But there are a lot of trick crowds that will not display any kind of pattern until halfway through the night, and they are difficult to play for," says Irene (71–72). Her helpful insight shows not just how delicately bands must move through the affective minefield of a dance floor, but also the way the ensemble negotiates between pattern and chaos, standard practice and mood swings, the canonical and the unex-pected. You can almost feel the bandleader's remembered desperation as she describes stock patterns of audience behavior, then the shock of unpredictability:

There are also clapping crowds who do not dance or anything, but all they do is sit and clap to you. . . . There are other crowds who dance and never clap, and you're never sure if you sound good. There are other places where people just listen like you're in a concert, but don't clap at all . . . the nondancing, nonclapping people are scary! (ibid:72)

The idea that a musician's relationship to his or her audience can be "scary" is an aspect of the inevitably commercial relationship of what I call *banding* here.

In *bonding*, the interplay is radically different. Take, for example, the Connecticut River valley tradition of ancient fife and drum corps. Pearce (1984:1) states: "These groups [are] usually associated with a township . . . drum corps men, women, and children have established themselves as a society complete with rituals, life cycle events, genealogies, and traditions. Usually organized by age and sex, they meet on a weekly basis." Unlike dance bands, they have "chaplains" who read a "company prayer" that includes lines such as "We thank you for the great company of Ancient musicians . . . we commend all who have marched before us into Your safe-keeping . . . we ask Your protection for fifers and drummers throughout the land" (11). In this simulated society, "babies teethe on drum sticks," and when the child is old enough, "he or she joins a junior unit." Romances among Ancient teenagers often culminate in marriage, a practice that is "vehemently encouraged by other Ancients." Finally, "many members are buried in uniform" (78–83).

The Ancient tradition serves to "turn the tables on the hyphenating of Americans," according to Pearce. Instead of splitting off into separate heritage-lines, Ancients—usually of Euro-American origin—amalgamate their varied pasts, using the old "melting pot" model, into a presumed "ancient" American patrimony of expressive culture. One handbook states: "Our antecedents may rest assured that the sounds of shrilling fifes and thundering drums are still to echo on and on" (91). While it is true that some form of fife and drum corps is as old as the American colonies, the Ancient tradition is an invented one in the classic style described by Hobsbawm and Ranger (1983). This is particularly evident in the case of formations like the Ancient Mariners, who stage pirate-style theatrical scenes along with their music-making. Certainly today's "musters," as group events are called, bear little resemblance either to the assembly of citizen-soldiers in American wars or to the factory bands of New England that also serve as a historical backdrop.

To a great extent, the Ancients are based in locale rather than heritage, each town producing a group that often bears more relationship to the high school marching-band model than to any eighteenth-century concept. Town and family ties, romance, drinking, and fun, combine in what Pearce calls "acceptable exhibitionism," as important here as history. All of these elements define a kind of social bonding that marks thousands of Euro-American ensembles. In a way, Pearce's Ancients seem most kin to Dundes and Falassi's (1975) *palio* fanatics in Siena, Italy, where the competition among city wards, centered on the annual horse-race, is even more microlocalized, and has been so for more centuries than the Connecticut drum corps have existed. Most bonding ensembles are not as extreme, being a kind of affinity group one can enter and leave at will as an isolated free agent, rather than as a member of a family or locale.

If the Ancients represent one end of a spectrum of bonding activity, Finnegan's (1989) British amateur musicians fall somewhere around the middle. Comfortable with the various traditions available in the newly developed town of Milton Keynes, they find what she calls "pathways" among forms as varied as classical ensemble, brass band, church choir, and jazz, pop, country-western, and rock bands. Here, bonding is both hereditary and environmental, personal and cultural, an implicit -scape of the local ecology. The oppositional, the purely arbitrary, and the "exotic," in terms of undescribed minority micromusics, seem airbrushed out of the picture.

I have little real argument with this portrait of Milton Keynes, not knowing the cultural climate firsthand, but I locate it somewhere between a tight, self-selected, *welded* sense of bonding visible in many micromusical scenes and, at the opposite end, a very loose, temporary, almost arbitrary affiliation, which I'll illustrate from another New England context, recent Sacred Harp singing groups, using Susan Garber's (1987) study: "Sacred Harp singing in New England is characterized by diversity. Participation cuts cross boundaries of age, sex, ethnicity and religion" to such an extent that the obviously religious basis of this old Protestant style "is one area of discomfort and disagreement among singers" (258). Though loosely based on a southern adaptation of an eighteenth-century New England style, the genre has gone through re-adaptation in its home region, a kind of revisionism that is "evidence of a growing attempt among singers to personalize the music" (257).

Garber's study is shot through with evidence of the "invention of tradition" as each newly formed group reinterprets an older style. Like the Ancients, Sacred Harp singers are aware of history, but not overly so; they are more interested in the excitement and immediacy of creating their own heritage from week to week. The resulting bonding occurs at several levels: (1) with a New England past, largely unknown but offering an aura of authenticity; (2) with recent southern practice, contacted directly by reciprocal visits between the regions; (3) with the emerging neo-New England tradition; as each northern group develops "a nature of its own, at the same time holding characteristics in common with other New England singings" (256). The urge to bond has moved rapidly across the literal and cultural landscape because of key activists and institutionalization. Folk music camps, public school workshops, college courses, church activities, museum performances, convalescent hospital visits, and even an appearance of a southern Sacred Harp leader in a Hollywood film have caused new roots to sprout from an old stump. All this has happened within a micromusical world that is no more than twenty years old.

The nature of this bonding is complex and somewhat indeterminate, some ensemble members being drawn by the mere sound and the possibility of fellowship, others making an analogy to familiar forms of Protestant singing. Yet despite these internal differences and the strong distinctions to be noticed among groups as disparate as black gospel choirs, the Ancients, British brass bands, and both southern and northern Sacred Harp groups, a common thread running right through the fabric of each is seen in many members' descriptions of such musical fellowships: the *transcendence* that live performance offers. The "quasi-trance state" one Vermont singer reports is shared by many members of affinity groups but is not commonly mentioned in interviews with dance band musicians.

John Bealle's study of "old-time" revivalist dancers in Indiana offers some support and some shadings. For these "old-time" dancers, Bealle (1988:177) cites as a basic organizing principle "euphoria as a transcendental ideology," related to Csikszentmihaly's general theory of "flow," a state of intense absorption, in human behavior. Yet Bealle points to nuances between what I call "banding" and "bonding" in the case of dancers who slowly drift into becoming dance callers and musicians. For these people and their dancer comrades, the line between the two activities is blurred as a monetary reward and a changed status of what Bealle calls "the expressive job" shift the participants' perspectives. At one extreme, a dancer "who enrolled in a Masters of Business Administration program reported less than empathetic reactions to the news of her enrollment" (239).

Ethnomusicology has long noticed the ensemble as a microcosm of expressive culture, or even as a metaphor for the social contract as a whole (Waterman 1990 being an excellent recent example), but Euro-American data have been noticeable largely by their absence. Yet particularly for subcultural music-making, the small performing group encompasses the full range of communal enterprise, from the mundane commercial life of the hired band through the transcendent fellowship of song, including links to local and intercultural industry, diasporic and intercultural contact networks, cross-subcultural rapport, and a sweeping sense of history that can bridge centuries or can almost instantaneously invent a tradition. De Tocqueville is often cited as pointing out the importance of voluntary associations for Americans as part of their national character, but it is hard to imagine that many of the benefits that performing ensembles offer are limited either to the United States or to the notion of democracy he defines so cogently. Surely one of the strengths of Soviet *samodeiatel'nost'* groups and the newer amateur singing circles of the various regions of the former USSR was their ability to tap the source of fellowship otherwise lacking in that society. Degteva, Boiko, and Burdzhi's (1984) poignant account of how displaced villagers and wartime buddies gathered in the parks of Moscow and then-Leningrad to play out literally their need for group performance tells us that the fellowship of music is well implanted across the whole of Euro-America. Early indications from the post-Soviet world show an efflorescence of the fellowship of song and dance as emerging nations reshape older patterns of belonging. Though subcultures live in the individual and in large collective acts like communal celebrations, a middle level of affiliation can often be the most intense, as well as analytically the most fruitful, sphere of lived experience.

Particularly salient moments occur at the intersection of banding and bonding, as on the dance floor. I have waved in the direction of this crucial meeting place above, but I would like to round out this chapter by taking a step closer to the juncture of those two collective components of micromusics, commerce and enthusiasm. Earlier on, I chastized José Limón for choosing to focus on the dancers in his *mexicano* club while scorning the musicians as too commodified to constitute a legitimate form of cultural expression. In his poetics, the passion of the dancers contrasts with the detachment of the band, yet I still feel that we cannot understand one group without the other. Those who study vernacular dance groups like contradancers (as opposed to the dancers in Arthur Murray studios) find that both the cohesion of the band and the coherence of the dance ensemble are problematic factors in analysis. Amateurism, among dancers and pick-up instrumentalists, and a presumed love for the style itself form the basis for the coexistence of the two types of performers who trek to the local grange hall on a weekend night. Professional dance callers take pains to sound folksy and to bridge the gap between the platform and the dance floor, while experienced dancers try to ignore the missteps of beginners. It is in the dynamics of such interaction of demarcated yet complementary groupings that the subculture emerges as a possible level of analysis, even while the superculture overarches a thousand dance floors through implicit constraints and permitted pathways.

The variable ways in which superculture and subculture play out their own dance here is richly complicated by the clearly intercultural connections of both banding and bonding in many Euro-American contexts, most of which reference histories that stretch beyond the immediate scene or places imagined or reconstructed for the here and now. It is not accidental that the Greek filmmaker Costas Ferris in his striking 1984 film *Rembetiko* uses a local band as a metaphor for the recent past of Greece, particularly stressing the intimate links between the individual singer and the collective ensemble, and their complete interpenetration with the communal "audience." The very opening sequence depicts the birth of the singer in a back room of the club, within earshot of both the band and its listeners, thus stressing total integration. Later devices include the familiar film trope of displaying the dates of passing years, which is backed up here by the band singing through verses of the same song, the music marking time, to suggest social stability in the midst of chaotic change. So dominant is the ensemble as a metaphor that the rather unmotivated, stagey killing of the singer at the end of the film is the only way the filmmaker can make his exit. Of particular interest for our purposes is the fluid movement between the individual—the singer—and the band, itself a shifting, competitive group of leaders and sidemen. The conflict of musical styles presented in *Rembetiko* also helps to make the film an almost ethnomusicological enterprise, even while its pretensions as allegory are all too apparent. The film reminds us that it may be too easy to equate the neighborhood ensemble with the larger society, but the energizing presence of a band in subcultural life cries out for closer attention.

Closing Thoughts

❖

Ending a work that stresses disjuncture, I would like to close this set of mini-essays by pointing out some gaps and cracks of my own. The point is not to disarm critics, but to suggest what else needs to be done to cover the field of micromusical studies I have outlined.

Some gaps are here because I did not have the data at hand to consider the many, many possible cases among the population of nearly one billion world citizens being surveyed (counting the former USSR). To take an egregious example, I know of scarcely any literature on the abundant micromusics of present-day France beyond those of the long-term regional/ethnic groups like the Bretons (for exceptions, see Mignon 1985 and Gross, McMurray, and Swedenburg 1992). Yet Paris is a major center for subcultural and intercultural musical commerce and creativity. Many other European countries are also absent from the discussion. Societies like those of the Netherlands and Denmark are slowly reconceptualizing themselves as heterogeneous, and colleagues there tell me that work will be forthcoming on subcultural contexts; I imagine that Italy cannot be far behind. In Portugal, a mixture of returned colonials and a variety of immigrants has created a musical mélange that is well worth investigating and probably soon will be studied.

It is beyond the concerns of this study to undertake an analysis of why there has been such reluctance in Western Europe to look inward, to appreciate the strength of subcultural expressive culture. The absence of music studies, however, is particularly striking when long-term, substantial funding has been available for transnational European research in areas like linguistics (for example, a multiyear investigation of "the ecology of second-language acquisition in adult immigrants" [see Perdue 1992]). Imagine how much richer my analysis could have been with the data from a similarly endowed multinational project with the word *music* instead of *language* in its title. Of course, the European funders are no more likely to think of music as a relevant variable in today's cultural pressure cooker than is the U.S. National Science Foundation. Lacking a firm basis in present practice, we cannot yet predict how the emerging relationships among the population groups of the European Community members will inflect the study of music or, for that matter, the practice. Questions such as whether power will devolve to Scotland significantly enough for local bands to slip further from mainstream British usage cannot be easily settled in advance, any more than we can foretell what the post-1992 integration of EC economies will do to the industrial interculture of music.

Beyond the boundaries of the European Community, I have been able to pay only limited attention to the former Eastern bloc nations and subnations. In the past, for obvious political reasons, there was little meaningful study of ethnic interaction or of the very intricate intercourse between center and periphery. A particularly fascinating area of research for the -cultures approach has arisen in the 1990s: the transition from subculture to superculture in the post-Soviet and post-Yugoslav regions, where groups that were once small embedded units within nation-states find themselves needing very quickly to develop their own national cultures as "former breakaway republics." Unfortunately, the formative stages of this period have already passed without significant attention being paid to the nuances of musical reformulation. To expand our base of knowledge of micromusics of the moment, I am working on a reader with contributions from European and American colleagues; some early findings from those studies are cited throughout the present volume. The coming decade should vastly expand our database for understanding issues that I have been able to raise only tentatively here.

For the United States, I am acutely aware of other sorts of gaps. For example, to the extent that I have subsumed material relating to the music of African-Americans, I have tended to talk about its intersections with other factors, such as class and, gender, as is often done today. In her pioneering study of "the sexual politics of women's blues," Hazel Carby (1986:9) says that her paper "focuses on black women as cultural producers and performers in the 1920s" while seeing their story as "part of a larger history of the production of Afro-American culture"; yet simultaneously she intends to "consider its marginality within a white dominated feminist discourse," thus offering a reasonable overlapping of planes of analysis.

An underlying question that this approach suggests is whether

African-American music should be treated like any other micromusic. I think there are some grounds for answering yes. One is suggested by the newly coined ethnonym itself, which ranks U.S. citizens of African descent as another diasporic community. There may be, however, compelling arguments for not doing so. The widespread preference by group members for the term *black* over *African-American* (72 percent to 15 percent, as of a January 1991 poll, according to the *New York Times*) should tell us that the people involved have very divided views on the subject. Basically, I feel that a comprehensive treatment of this complex situation lies beyond the scope of the present work and of my research competence, particularly since the issue is now tied to a broader, emerging American tendency to distinguish between "people of color" and other types of subcultures. This movement itself is part of a process of restless redefinition of standard approaches to group identity, including those based on gender and sexual preference as well as heritage, with strong implications for the evolution of micromusics. I believe that it is too soon to incorporate these fast-moving trends into an analysis of contemporary societies.

Paul Gilroy has made a helpful move in new directions by pointing out the weaknesses of most current polemics on the subject of black music: ". . . the unashamedly hybrid character of these black cultures continually confounds any simplistic (essentialist or anti-essentialist) understanding of the relationship between racial identity and racial non-identity, between folk cultural authenticity and pop cultural betrayal." More specifically, he zeroes in on the problem we cultural critics face in defining positions:

Music and its rituals can be used to create a model where by identity can be understood neither as a fixed essence nor as a vague and utterly contingent construction to be reinvented by the will and whim of aesthetes, symbolists, and language gamers (Gilroy 1992:np).

But exactly how that model will be constructed remains elusive at present.

Part of the reason for my reluctance lies in the specifics, if not vagaries, of local understandings and definitions. For example, as an American, I was taken aback by an anthology called *Black Music in Britain* (Oliver 1990), which included music of South Asian immigrants. British colleagues tell me that this terminology was part of a tactical move in their society, which made sense for a time, but which is now somewhat dated. The weakness of any comparative insight is, of course, the impossibility of taking both global generality and local specificity into account. Along those lines, I have also been reluctant to make separate arguments for indigenous peoples, refugees, guest workers, members of long-standing regional/national groups, and other such categories despite recent, quite cogent suggestions to do so (Schramm 1989; Hirshberg 1989). These exclusions are a necessary part of comparativism, the price we pay for trying to identify common features among micromusics, which I think specialized perspectives tend to overlook in favor of distinctiveness, that idol of ethnography. Whether my proposed discourse of commonalities can charm methodology away from its fascination with group particularity is up to the reader. As I said at the outset, the point here is not to arrive at a solution, but to raise questions, mostly about rethinking units of analysis.

A logical, related question is to what extent questions raised here can be transferred to other world regions. I would not presume to answer so large a question, but while reading the conclusion to Veit Erlmann's thought-provoking *African Stars: Studies in Black South African Performance*, two quotations leaped out at me that might indicate a certain overlap. One shows how complex an issue class is becoming, a subject I wrangled with above: "In Durban, for instance, black residents may have perceived class-based distinctions in their performance activities, but the analysis of recorded material reveals that virtually all sectors of the city's black population drew on the same stock of musical techniques and practices" (Erlmann 1991:179). Here the disjuncture between class as an insider's intuition versus an outsider's category stands out sharply. It is further problematized within a particularly complex society as part of a cluster of issues involving race, migration patterns, active intervention of the recording industry, and lively intercultural interaction with North America, all issues of central importance to understanding Euro-America itself. The second quotation follows almost immediately: "The most useful insight then to be gained for the ethnomusicologist and social historian from the South African evidence is the need to situate the development and ideology of modern performance styles within a network of fluctuating group relations." Change the geographical reference and the sentence could stand as an epigraph for the present study.

Any neat scheme to organize the inherently volatile, constantly shifting world of today's expressive cultures can offer only one perspective on a multidimensional scene. I tested out a model based on "visibility" in chapter 1; to conclude, let me offer another such tripartite approach, threefold thinking being endemic in Euro-America. My work in Afghanistan started me off on an idea that blossomed later when I viewed "the West," namely, that there are three types of situations of intergroup contact—long-standing, medium-range, and quite recent.

To take Euro-American examples, the Finns and the Swedes, or the French and the Bretons, have had to deal with each other in complex ways for a very long time, creating a situation of musical contact that is spread out leisurely over a *longue durée* that might require a certain methodology. Looking at the Eastern European Jews in the United States, on the other hand, only becomes an issue after 1881, when they arrive in very large numbers and swamp the already established category of Jewish-Americans. One has a few generations' worth of data to deal with rather than a few centuries.

The third type of situation can be represented by the Turks or Yugoslavs and the Swedes in Stockholm, or the contact between African-Americans and Korean-Americans in New York or Los Angeles, where the 1970s are the formative period. The fact that both Swedish and American laws and bureaucracies have been struggling to take account of the rights and responsibilities of newly emerging small groups shows that issues arising in the short term may require special attention. Shifts in immigration law may bring about unprecedented situations that may impact music, as for example the recent American governmental tendency to welcome middle-class immigrants. At the local level, it was not until the 1980s that Asian-American college students have constituted enough of a presence on campuses to refocus cultural politics, including music. Only in the 1990s could a transplanted Indian filmmaker like Meera Nair find meaningful musical ways to code small-town African-American and Indian-American communities in the movie *Mississippi Masala* (1992); the film includes, surprisingly but cogently, the intercultural ties of both groups to Africa (the Indians having been uprooted from Uganda). Sometimes just the exercise of visualizing relationships in terms of length of contact can clarify certain issues of interaction.

The problems with this rather neat, surprisingly helpful perspective are obvious and multiple; I will cite only the most salient for present purposes. The tripartite model just sketched completely elides the overarching categories suggested in this volume, according to which we could identify the constant processes of supercultural, subcultural, and intercultural interaction that inform all three levels. Nair still uses the stock blues harmonica as the principal code for southern blacks, and the foil for both depicted minorities is still the local dominant white "cracker" culture, whose hegemonic control is illustrated in the film. Central authority and local style have been in interaction in somewhat similar ways across the various *durées* suggested above, as has the tendency of an embedded group to reach out to relatives beyond immediate frontiers. In some ways, the length of contact time is illusory, while in other ways, it opens a particular window on intergroup contact that allows us to get a better look into certain rooms. Both approaches, then, are comparative and offer particular types of insight. Either might help us to notice that an important innovative aspect of *Mississippi Masala* is its showcasing of an inter-subcultural dynamic, so rarely the concern of mainstream cinema, yet that the presentation of each group is always done through standardized musical coding, which the film carries out with almost dogged consistency. At the present, I am more drawn to the bird's-eye view of the -cultures perspective, though that vantage point always has a certain panoptic quality that might be a liability at times. That is, arranging everyone's musical life under the analyst's infallible gaze can also create a mirage, and perhaps a somewhat oppressive one. As always, I recommend carrying a number of lenses in the observer's camera bag, and of course turning over the apparatus to the subject frequently to guarantee a reverse shot, something else I was all too rarely able to do in this extended essay, essentially my own reflections.

Finally, the ambiguity of music makes a mockery of any snapshot philosophy, clean categorization, neat nesting of levels, or sense of analytical closure. I am convinced that this is the reason the composer Shostakovich survived when the poet Mandelstam perished under Stalin: as decadent and difficult as music might sound, a potentially subversive message could never quite be deciphered, nor did it matter quite as much as a questionable poem. Much closer to home, today's newspaper (*Santa Cruz Sentinel*, March 11, 1992) brings the multivalence of music into immediate focus in an Associated Press account of a conservative pundits' meeting on the export of American popular culture. Judge Robert Bork says that pop culture is "trashing American values" and that its proponents have "a nihilistic hatred of America as it exists today," while Walter Berns, a professor at Georgetown University, insists that "in a better world we would require Madonna to clean up her act—we used to do that until about 30 years ago." However, while Berns would like to censor pop music at home, he is in favor of exporting it—but in recorded form only, for he proposes to restrict the movements of "the musicians themselves, the rockers, the rappers and all the Madonnas." This deeply ambivalent attitude among the group extends to Irving Kristol's celebration of American popular culture, which "has a wonderfully corrosive effect on all totalitarian and strongly authoritarian regimes" because of its individualistic/anarchic quality. Yet another speaker proudly rattles off the impressive statistics of cultural export, citing his sighting of an Eddie Murphy movie in Bhutan as a particularly telling example of the triumph of the American Way.

When ideologues can display such a spectrum of opinion on musical materials, how can academic relativists agree on the meaning of, or even a methodology for, the songs that surround us? The conservatives' wandering from the aura of the star through the industrial infrastructure of distribution to the textual analysis of song lyrics or back to the body language of live performance displays the type of level-shifting and generalized hunt for units of analysis I have noted as endemic to our academic discourse. In the same roundtable, Ben Wattenberg even adds the historical dimension, pointing out that Rome is better remembered because "we speak its language and follow its law" than because it achieved economic success; thus we should look positively at America's cultural dominance. How many of us have not been tempted by century-crossing to anchor today's musical meanings in yesterday's contexts?

Like other intellectuals, the Heritage Foundation specialists just cited have noted the importance of global cultural flow, the preeminence of the popular music/dance complex as an export of both industry and ideology, and the internal paradox of a commerce built on romantic individualism but expressing corporate control. Where they differ from left-wing analysts is in their prescriptive interest in finding means to channel the energy of music, restricting its communicability to the industrial object (recording) to be decoded at a safe distance from its source in America, and simultaneously curbing the very freewheeling performance mode that makes the export item a viable commodity. In attempting to reconcile these inbuilt complementarities, if not contradictions, of music, the right-wing pundits will succeed no better in practice than cultural studies proponents have done in theory. I remain impressed by music's stubborn resistance to reduction; it will survive all our efforts at intellectual control. At the same time, the voices and the songs of the millions of deterritorialized, or simply troubled, citizens of Euro-America will continue to force us to focus on the very human reasons for the greatly increasing importance of music in our times, spurring us not to reduce, but constantly to reimagine, to reevaluate, and to come to grips with the power of music as the voice of a people, however defined, marketed, analyzed, and digitally sampled that voice might be. I suppose I am only urging us both to think globally and to act locally, as current slogans have it, but also as our own intellectual traditions might urge us. It seems the least we can do.

Bibliography

❖

Abu-Lughod, Lila. 1986. *Veiled Sentiments: Honor and Poetry in a Bedouin Society*. NY: Oxford University Press.
———. 1991. "Writing against Culture." In Fox 1991, 137–62.
Alekseev, Eduard. 1988. *Fol'klor v kontekste sovremennoi kul'tury*. Moscow: Sovetskii kompozitor.
Altman, R., and M. Kaufman. 1971. *The Making of a Musical*. New York: Crown.
Anderson, Benedict. 1983. *Imagined Communities: Reflections on the Origin and Spread of Nationalism*. London: Verso.
Anzaldúa, Gloria. 1990. "Taming the Wild Tongue." In *Out There: Marginalization and Contemporary Cultures*, edited by R. Ferguson et al., 203–12. Cambridge: MIT Press.
Appadurai, Arjun. 1990. "Disjuncture and Difference in the Global Cultural Economy." *Public Culture* 2(2): 1–24.
———. 1991. "Global Ethnoscapes: Notes and Queries for a Transnational Anthropology." In Fox 1991, 191–210.
Applegate, Jane. 1989. "Pepsi Recruits Madonna to Help Fight Cola War." *Los Angeles Times*, January 26.
Averill, Gage. 1990. "Four Parts, No Waiting: The Ideal of Male Camaraderie in Barbershop Harmony." Paper delivered at the Thirty-fifth Annual Convention, Society for Ethnomusicology.
Baily, John. 1990. "Qawwali in Bradford: Traditional Music in a Muslim Community." In Oliver 1990, 153–65.
Banerji, Sabita, and Gerd Baumann. 1990. "Bhangra 1984–8: Fusion and Professionalization in a Genre of South Asian Dance Music." In Oliver 1990, 137–52.
Barber-Kersovan, Alenka. 1989. "Tradition and Acculturation as Polarities of Slovenian Popular Music." In Frith 1989, 73–89.
Barthes, Roland. 1981. *Camera Lucida: Reflections on Photography*. New York: Hill and Wang.
Baxandall, Michael. 1985. *Patterns of Intention: On the Historical Explanation of Pictures*. New Haven: Yale University Press.
Bealle, John. 1988. "American Folklore Revival: A Study of an Old-Time Music and Dance Community." Ph.D. dissertation, Indiana University.
Becker, Howard. 1982. *Artworlds*. Berkeley and Los Angeles: University of California Press.

Bolle-Zemp, Sylvie. 1990. "Institutionalized Folklore and Helvetic Ideology." *Yearbook for Traditional Music* 22:127–40.

Bourdieu, Pierre. 1984. *Distinction: A Social Critique of the Judgement of Taste*. Cambridge: Harvard University Press.

Browne, David. 1990. "The Music Business Watches its Own Step." *New York Times*, September 23.

Bushnell, John. 1990. *Moscow Grafitti: Language and Subcultures*. Boston: Unwin Hyman.

Carby, Hazel. 1986. "It Just Be's Dat Way Sometime: The Sexual Politics of Women's Blues." *Radical America* 20(4): 9–22.

Chapman, M., M. McDonald and E. Tonkin, eds. 1989. *History and Ethnicity*. London: Routledge.

Clarke, Gary. 1990. "Defending Ski-jumpers: A Critique of Theories of Youth Subcultures." In *On Record*, edited by S. Frith and A. Goodwin, 81–96. New York: Pantheon.

Clifford, James. 1990. "Traveling Selves, Traveling Others." Talk delivered at "Cultural Studies Now and in the Future" conference, Champaign-Urbana, April 5–9.

Cowan, Jane. 1990. *Dance and the Body Politic in Northern Greece*. Princeton: Princeton University Press.

de Certeau, Michel. 1984. *The Practice of Everyday Life*. Berkeley: University of California Press.

Degteva, N.; Y. Boiko and F. Burdzhi. 1984. "Fenomen bytovoi kul'tury sovremmenogo goroda—parkovyi piatachok." In Zemtsovski 1984, 54–79.

Dundes, Alan, and A. Falassi. 1975. *La Terra in Piazza: An Interpretation of the Palio of Siena*. Berkeley and Los Angeles: University of California Press.

Erlmann, Veit. 1991. *African Stars: Studies in Black South African Performance*. Chicago and London: University of Chicago Press.

Fabbri, Franco. 1989. "The System of *Canzone* in Italy Today." In Frith 1989, 122–42.

Faulkner, Robert R. 1983. *Music on Demand: Composers and Careers in the Hollywood Film Industry*. New Brunswick and London: Transaction Books.

Finnegan, Ruth. 1989. *The Hidden Musicians: Music-Making in an English Town*. Cambridge: Cambridge University Press.

Fiske, John. 1989. *Understanding Popular Culture*. Boston: Unwin Hyman.

Fox, Richard G., ed. 1991. *Recapturing Anthropology: Working in the Present*. Santa Fe: School of American Research Press.

Frith, Simon. 1988. "Video Pop: Picking up the Pieces." In *Facing the Music*, edited by S. Frith, 88–130. New York: Pantheon.

Frith, Simon, ed. 1989. *World Music, Politics, and Social Change*. Manchester and New York: Manchester University Press.

Gal, Susan. 1988. "The Political Economy of Code Choice." In Heller 1988: 245–64.

Garber, Susan. 1987. "The Sacred Harp Revival in New England: Its Singers and Singings." M.A. thesis, Wesleyan University.

Gilroy, Paul. 1987. *There Ain't No Black in the Union Jack*. London: Hutchinson.

———. 1992. Excerpts from "Sounds Authentic: Black Music, Ethnicity, and the Challenge of a *Changing* Same," in *Center for Cultural Studies Newsletter*, Spring 1992. Santa Cruz: University of California (not paginated).

Gitlin, Todd. 1983. *Inside Prime Time*. New York: Pantheon.

Glasser, Ruth. 1990. "Paradoxical Ethnicity: Puerto Rican Musicians in Post World War I New York City." *Latin American Music Review* 11(1): 63–72.

Godmilow, Jill. 1976. *The Popovich Brothers of South Chicago*. Film produced by the Balkan Arts Center.

Gold, Gerald, ed. 1984. *Minorities and Mother Country Imagery*. St. John's: Memorial University of Newfoundland.

Gross, Joan, David McMurray, and Ted Swedenburg. 1992. "Arab Noise, World Beat, and the F.I.S. Wave: the Articulation of Rai Music in its Franco-Maghrebi, Diasporic, American and Algerian Contexts," forthcoming in *Diaspora*.

Guilbault, Jocelyne. 1990. "Cultural, Social, and Economic Development through Music; Zouk in the French Antilles." Unpublished paper.

Hall, Stuart. 1991. "The Question of Identity." Talk given at the University of California, Santa Cruz, March 21.

Hall, S., and T. Jefferson, eds. 1975. *Resistance through Rituals*. London: Hutchinson.

Haraszti, Miklos. 1987. *The Velvet Prison: Artists under State Socialism*. New York: Basic Books.

Hebdige, Dick. 1979. *Subculture: The Meaning of Style*. London: Methuen.

Heisler, Martin O. 1990. "Ethnicity and Ethnic Relations in the Modern West." In *Conflict and Peacemaking in Multiethnic Societies*, edited by J. Montville, 23–52. Lexington, Mass. and Toronto: D. C. Heath.

Heller, Monica, ed. 1988. *Codeswitching: Anthropological and Sociolinguistic Perspectives*. Berlin: Mouton de Gruyter.

Herndon, M., and Ziegler, S., eds. 1990. *Music, Gender, and Culture*. Wilhelmshaven: Florian Noetzel.

Hirshberg, Jehoash. 1989. "The Role of Music in the Renewed Self-Identity of Karaite Jewish Refugee Communities from Cairo." *Yearbook for Traditional Music* 21: 36–54.

Hobsbawm, E., and T. Ranger, eds. 1983. *The Invention of Tradition*. Cambridge: Cambridge University Press.

Horovitz, Bruce. 1989. "Pepsi Plans No New Ads to Sub for Pulled Madonna TV Spot." *Los Angeles Times*, April 20.

Hymes, Dell. 1974. "Ways of Speaking." In *Explorations in the Ethnography of Speaking*, edited by R. Bauman and J. Sherzer, 433–52. New York and London: Cambridge University Press.

Kealiinohomoku, Joann W. 1986. "The Would-Be Indian." In *Explorations in Ethnomusicology: Essays in Honor of David P. McAllester*, edited by C. Frisbie, 111–26. Detroit: Detroit Monographs in Musicology.

Keefe, Susan E., and Amado M. Padilla. 1987. *Chicano Ethnicity*. Albuquerque: University of New Mexico Press.

Keil, Charles. 1982. "Slovenian Style in Milwaukee." In *Folk Music and Modern Sound*, edited by W. Ferris and S. Hart, 32–59. Oxford: University of Mississippi Press.

Keil, C. and A. Keil. 1984. "In Pursuit of Polka Happiness." *Musical Traditions* 2: 6–11.

Klassen, Doreen Helen. 1989. *Singing Mennonite: Low German Songs among the Mennonites*. Winnipeg: University of Manitoba Press.

Klymasz, Robert. 1972. "Sounds You Never Heard Before: Ukrainian Country Music in Western Canda." *Ethnomusicology* 16(3): 372–80.

Koskoff, Ellen. 1978. "Contemporary Nigun Composition in an American Hasidic Community." In Porter 1978, 153–74.

———. 1982. "The Music-Network: A Model for the Organization of Music Concepts. *Ethnomusicology* 26(3): 353–70.

————. 1987. *Women and Music in Cross-Cultural Perspective*. Urbana: University of Illinois Press.

————. 1991. "Gender, Power, and Music." In *The Musical Woman: Volume III, 1986–1990*, edited by Judith L. Zaimont, 769–88. New York: Greenwood Press.

Labov, William. 1972. *Sociolinguistic Patterns*. Philadelphia: University of Pennsylvania Press.

Larkey, Edward. 1989. "Ethnicity and Cultural Policies: Popular Music in the German-Speaking Countries." Paper delivered at the Thirty-fourth Annual Convention, Society for Ethnomusicology.

Leary, James. 1984. "Old Time Music in Northern Wisconsin." *American Music* 2:1, 71–87.

————. 1986. *Accordions in the Cutover: Field Recordings of Ethnic Music from Lake Superior's South Shore*. Northland, Minn.: Northland College.

————. 1987. "Reading the 'Newspaper Dress': An Exposé of Art Moilanen's Musical Tradition." In *Michigan Folklife Reader*, edited by C. Dewhurst and Y. Lockwood, 205–23. E. Lansing: Michigan State University.

Limón, José E. 1991. "Representation, Ethnicity, and the Precursory Ethnography: Notes of a Native Anthropologist." In Fox 1991, 115–36.

Lippard, Lucy. 1990. *Mixed Blessings: New Art in a Multicultural America*. New York: Pantheon.

Lipsitz, George. 1990. *Time Passages: Collective Memory and American Popular Culture*. Minneapolis: University of Minnesota Press.

McAllester, D., and C. Frisbie. 1984. *Navajo Blessingway Singer: The Autobiography of Frank Mitchell: 1881–1967*. Tucson: University of Arizona Press.

McHale, Ellen. 1981. "French Canadian to Franco-American: A Study of the Music Culture of Derby, Vermont." M.A. thesis, Wesleyan University.

MacLeod, Bruce. 1979. "Music for All Occasions." Ph.D. dissertation, Wesleyan University.

Manuel, Peter. 1988. *Popular Music of the Non-Western World*. Oxford: Oxford University Press.

Middleton, Richard. 1990. *Studying Popular Music*. Milton Keynes: Open University Press.

Mignon, Patrick. 1985. "Enquete: la musique et les Beurs," in *Vibrations* 1, 137–66.

Nettl, Bruno. 1983. *The Study of Ethnomusicology*. Urbana: University of Illinois Press.

Niles, Christina. 1978. "The Revival of the Latvian Kokle in America." In Porter 1978, 211–39.

Oliver, Paul, ed. 1990. *Black Music in Britain: Essays on the Afro-Asian Contribution to Popular Music*. Buckingham: Open University Press.

Paredes, Americo. 1958. *"With his Pistol in his Hand": A Border Ballad and its Hero*. Austin: University of Texas Press.

Pareles, Jon. 1992. "The Disappearance of Ice-T's 'Cop Killer.'" *New York Times* July 30, C13.

Pearce, Nancy. 1984. "The Ancient Fife and Drum Culture of the Connecticut River Valley." B.A. thesis, Wesleyan University.

Peña, Manuel. 1985. *The Texas-Mexican Conjunto: History of a Working-Class Music*. Austin: University of Texas Press.

Perdue, C. 1992. *The Cross-Linguistic Study of Second Languages*. Cambridge: Cambridge University Press.

Poplack, Shana. 1988. "Contrasting Patterns of Code-Switching in Two Communities." In Heller 1988, 215–44.

Porter, James, ed. 1978. *Euro-American Traditional Music*. UCLA Selected Reports in Ethnomusicology 3(1).

Pred, Allan. 1990. *Lost Words and Lost Worlds: Modernity and the Language of Everyday Life in Late Nineteenth-Century Stockholm*. Cambridge: Cambridge University Press.

Randel, Don M. 1991. "Crossing over with Rubén Blades." *Journal of the American Musicological Society* 44(2), 301–32.

Ronström, Owe. 1989. "Making Use of History: The Revival of the Bagpipe in Sweden in the 1980s." *Yearbook for Traditional Music* 21:95–108.

Ryback, Timothy. 1990. *Rock around the Bloc: A History of Rock Music in Eastern Europe and the Soviet Union*. New York: Oxford University Press.

Sacks, Oliver. 1984. *A Leg to Stand On*. New York: Summit Books.

———. 1987. *The Man Who Mistook His Wife for a Hat*. New York: Harper and Row.

———. 1992. "The Last Hippie." *New York Review of Books* 39(6) (March 26): 53–61.

Schneider, Jo Anne. 1990. "Defining Boundaries, Creating Contacts: Puerto Rican and Polish Representation of Group Identity through Ethnic Parades." *Journal of Ethnic Studies* 18(1): 33–57.

Schramm, Adelaida Reyes. 1989. "Music and Tradition: From Native to Adopted Land through the Refugee Experience." *Yearbook for Traditional Music* 21:25–35.

Schuyler, Philip. 1984. "Berber Professional Musicians in Performance." In *Performance Practice: Ethnomusicological Perspectives*, edited by G. Béhague, 91–148. NY: Greenwood Press.

Simmel, Georg. 1955. "Conflict" and "The Web of Group-Affiliations." Translated by K. Wolff and R. Bendix. New York: The Free Press.

Slobin, Mark. 1979. *Code Switching and Code Superimposition in Music*. Working Papers in Sociolinguistics, no. 63.

———. 1983. "Rethinking 'Revival' of American Ethnic Music." *New York Folklore* 9(3–4): 38–43.

———. 1986. "Multilingualism in Folk Music Cultures." In *Explorations in Ethnomusicology: Essays in Honor of David P. McAllester*, edited by C. Frisbie, 3–10. Detroit: Detroit Monographs in Musicology.

———. 1988. "Icons of Ethnicity: Pictorial Themes in Commercial Euro-American Music." *Imago Musicae*, 129–43.

———. 1990a. *Chosen Voices: The Story of the American Cantorate*. Urbana: University of Illinois Press.

———. 1990b. "Engendering the Cantorate." *YIVO Annual* 19:147–68.

———. 1992. "Micromusics of the West: A Comparative Approach." *Ethnomusicology* 36:1 (January 1987).

Slobin, Mark, and Richard Spottswood, 1984. "David Medoff: A Case Study in Interethnic Popular Culture." *American Music* 3(3): 261–76.

Sommers, Laurie Kay. 1991. "Inventing Latinismo: The Creation of 'Hispanic' Panethnicity in the United States. *Journal of American Folklore* 104:32–53.

Spalding, Mary. 1986. "The Irene Olszewski Orchestra: A Connecticut Band." M.A. thesis, Wesleyan University.

Starr, Frederick. 1980. *Red and Hot: The Fate of Jazz in the Soviet Union, 1917–1980*. New York: Oxford University Press.

Troitsky, Artemy. 1987. *Back in the USSR: The True Story of Rock in Russia*. Boston and London: Faber.

Vander, Judith. 1989. *Songprints*. Champaign: University of Illinois Press.

Wallis, R. and K. Malm. 1984. *Big Music from Small Countries*. New York: Pendragon Press.

Waterman, Christopher. 1990. "'Our Tradition Is a Very Modern Tradition': Popular Music and the Construction of Yoruba Identity." *Ethnomusicology* 34(3): 367–80.

Waters, Mary. 1990. *Ethnic Options*. Berkeley and Los Angeles: University of California Press.

Weiss, Michael. 1988. *The Clustering of America*. New York: Harper and Row.

Welk, Lawrence. 1971. *Wunnerful, Wunnerful! The Autobiography of Lawrence Welk*. Englewood Cliffs, N.J.: Prentice-Hall.

White, Anne. 1990. *De-stalinization and the House of Culture*. New York and London: Routledge.

Williams, Raymond. 1977. *Marxism and Literature*. Oxford: Oxford University Press.

Zemtsovski, Izali, ed. 1984. *Traditsionnyi fol'klor v sovremennoi khudozhestvennoi zhizni*. Leningrad: LGITMiK.2.

Zheng, Su de San. 1990. "Soft Boundaries and Situational Strategies: A Chinese Immigrant Music Group in New York City." Manuscript.

Index

❖

UNIVERSITY PRESS OF NEW ENGLAND publishes books under its own imprint and is the publisher for Brandeis University Press, Brown University Press, University of Connecticut, Dartmouth College, Middlebury College Press, University of New Hampshire, University of Rhode Island, Tufts University, University of Vermont, and Wesleyan University Press.

ABOUT THE AUTHOR

Mark Slobin is Professor of Music at Wesleyan University. Among his books are *Chosen Voices: The Story of the American Cantorate* (1989), *Tenement Songs: The Popular Music of the Jewish Immigrants* (1982), *Music in the Culture of Northern Afghanistan* (1976), and *Kirgiz Instrumental Music* (1969).

Library of Congress Cataloging-in-Publication Data

Slobin, Mark.
Subcultural sounds : micromusics of the West / Mark Slobin.
    p.   cm. (Music / Culture)
"Earlier version . . . published as 'Micromusics of the West: a comparative approach' in Ethnomusicology, 36/1, (Winter 1992)"—T.p. verso.
Includes bibliographical references and index.
ISBN 0–8195–5253–4 (cl). — ISBN 0–8195–6261–0 (pa)
    1. Ethnomusicology.   I. Title.
ML3798.S46   1993
780'.89–dc20   92–34289
        ∞   MN